RATNER SCHOOLS
4900 ANDERSON ROAD
LYNDHURST, OHIO 44124

THIS MY PEOPLE

OTHER BOOKS BY THE AUTHOR

Indian Sculpture in Bronze and Stone

India, Painting from Ajanta Caves

Indian Miniatures

Ajanta, Painting of the Sacred and the Secular

Himalayan Art

The White Horse

First published in the United States of America in 1990 by
RIZZOLI INTERNATIONAL PUBLICATIONS, INC.
300 Park Avenue South, New York, NY 10010

ISBN 0-8478-1153-0
LC 89-61766

Printed and bound in Italy by Amilcare Pizzi s.p.a., Cinisello Balsamo, Milan.

THIS MY PEOPLE

HAND-WRITTEN PREFACE
JAWAHARLAL NEHRU

FOREWORD
RAJIV GANDHI

TEXT AND PHOTOGRAPHS
MADANJEET SINGH

RIZZOLI
NEW YORK

Plate 1:   JAWAHARLAL NEHRU, PHOTOGRAPHED AT TEEN MURTI HOUSE ON THE DAY HE WROTE THE PREFACE TO *THIS MY PEOPLE*

India is frequently represented by pictures of its noble buildings and its famous monuments of antiquity. Sometimes we see more modern structures, which may be impressive in their own way, but are seldom noted for their grace or beauty.

We have also pictures of her mountains and lakes and forests, and vast plains, and great rivers and raging torrents and bubbling brooks.

All that is India, or a part of India. It is impossible to compress the infinite variety of India in a book or in a collection of pictures.

Latterly, the politicians of India appear almost daily in some pose or other in the newspapers. They compete, in this respect, with the film stars of other countries. It is not a happy development. But that too is India.

Then we have pictures of parties and receptions, especially in New Delhi, with the same people, or more or less the same people, going from one reception to another. They represent the official world as well as the non-officials of note and substance, with their wives and daughters. That too is India.

But here in this volume there is a different aspect of India — the common folk, the masses, the people. Again, they represent some odd types chosen from Kashmir in the North to Kanya Kumari in the far South. It might have been possible to choose an entirely different set of types and they would have been equally representative of this rather wonderful country of ours. But this set of pictures does give an idea of our people in the humbler ranks of society. The pictures are good and I hope that many will derive pleasure from them and some understanding, as I have done.

Jawaharlal Nehru

New Delhi – January 9, 1949

FOREWORD

I am glad Madanjeet Singh has snatched back this fragment of history from the drawers of his writing desk, where the manuscript has languished for close on four decades. It is an intensely personal account of an epochal event in the life of the nation, the tumultuous joy of independence, the agony of partition, the thrill of nationbuilding.

It is also a memoir that etches one of the greatest personalities of our time, Jawaharlal Nehru, from the perspective of a sensitive young artist who finds his growing into manhood coinciding with his country growing out of bondage, into freedom and liberty.

The theme of the book, of both the photographs and the text, is the great running theme of our ancient civilization; unity in diversity, the celebration of that multifaceted heterogeneity that distinguishes our civilization from most others, the recognition that there is so much that is wondrous, wise and beautiful on this earth that our windows should be open to the best of all that blows in from wherever it blows. Out of this recognition comes tolerance and compassion showing the path to truth and nonviolence, one humanity and one world.

New Delhi   March 14, 1989

Plate 2:   CHILDREN IN A WHEAT FARM, NILGIRI HILLS

Plate 3:
NATI, TENTH CENTURY A.D., SRIRANGAM

THIS MY PEOPLE

It seems like yesterday. One fine winter morning in the first week of January 1949, I picked up my bicycle, tied on its rack an album of photographs, and took off for Teen Murti House, the residence of the Prime Minister of India. In my youthful exuberance, the outlandish idea I had was to meet with Jawaharlal Nehru himself, and request him to write a preface to *This My People*, a collection of the photographs I had compiled during the preceding three years.

At the time, I was staying with Gurbaksh Singh, the distinguished editor of *Preet Lari*. He had been obliged to abandon his home in the Punjab because Preet Nagar, the flourishing commune he had founded near Amritsar and where his journal was originally published, happened to fall right on the Indian border with the newly created Pakistan. Like most refugees, he had until the last moment tenaciously resisted being uprooted from his soil and then had wandered in the wilderness until he found temporary refuge in a rather dilapidated building at Mehrauli. The *kothi* seemed as old as Qutub Minar, the famous tower which I could see through a termite-eaten wooden window of my dingy room on the upper floor. On this level Gurbaksh Singh occupied three rooms with his wife and six children, while on the ground floor, his printing press was trying desperately to prevent the Punjabi magazine *The Garland of Love* from closing down because of dwindling subscriptions. The sprawling hamlet in Preet Nagar, the life-time ambition he had so painstakingly realized over the years, had shrunk into a shack of two floors, but never his spirit that conceived the *Township of Love*.

Urbanization had yet to invade Mehrauli, a sleepy village on the outskirts of New Delhi. Without a proper motor road, the distances on a bicycle seemed even greater than they actually were. So I had risen at daybreak and, while everyone was asleep, I washed myself, tied my turban, and tiptoed out of the house, in the hope of meeting with Panditji before he went to the office at about nine o'clock. It was a chilly morning, and I could not tell whether the shiver I felt passing down my spine was because of the cold or nervousness. The Qutub Minar stood across the road in all its splendour as the radiant crimson light of the rising sun illuminated its red stones, making the tower glow all the more in its phosphorescent rays. Ascending towards the clear, transparent sky was a soft mist that rose from the sparkling dew on the lawns and flower-beds — an ethereal vapour that seemed to lift the massive tower magically into the air. Not far from the low brick wall surrounding the park, a group of peasants were tending their cows and buffaloes. They were muffled in misty puffs of smog, smelling of the peculiar odour of burning cow dung, as the women were lighting fires in the open. Against the spreading sunlight from the opposite direction, the shadows of their figures were outlined in a silky softness, and I stood there looking at the scene for some time as the silhouettes of farmers and their cattle in the hazy atmosphere reminded me of the day when I was set free from prison during the Quit India movement.

Some events and experiences of the past are so charged with emotion that they spontaneously come back to life whenever the surroundings and the senses with which they were initially associated are evoked. A foggy environment of this kind invariably brought back to my mind that marvellous day when a group of farmers had smuggled me and a group of my colleagues out of the clutches of the police who wanted to re-arrest us, soon after we were released from Mirzapur jail. As we were making a dash for freedom, I had similarly seen in the milky vapour ascending towards the sky, some beautiful silhouettes of a herd of cattle being driven home by a cowherd. Suddenly the claustrophobia of the high prison walls that had suffocated me for nearly a year had vanished, and in this fantastic panorama of liberty, my head swam with overwhelming happiness. I felt within me a bewildering force, an inward flowering of joy that comes from the grace of awakening to a new life. Thus the emotional ecstasy I sensed on that first day of freedom seemed to have become visually associated with the mysterious veil of mist that I had then seen hovering over the steaming landscape of the United Provinces, as Uttar Pradesh was then called. As I pedalled towards New Delhi along the narrow road that passed through swaying fields of sugar-cane, the fresh air gently caressing my face recalled an invigorating breeze which had produced a similar sense of euphoria on that day.

I was confident that Pandit Nehru would be interested in my photographs of the people, as the subject was close to his heart. In a passage I had read once again in "my bible", *The Discovery of India,* he seemed to articulate my own feelings. In this remarkable book, which he wrote in Ahmadnagar Fort prison during the Quit India movement, he had described some of his impressions about the people with acute sensitivity: "I looked at their faces and their figures and watched their movements. There was many a sensitive face and many a sturdy

10

Plates 5a and 5b: LANDSCAPE, MAHARASHTRA ▶

body, straight and clean-limbed; and among the women there was grace and suppleness and dignity and poise, and very often a look that was full of melancholy. Sometimes, as I was passing along a country road or through a village, I would start with surprise on seeing a fine type of man or a beautiful woman, who reminded me of some fresco of ancient times. And I wondered how the type endured and continued through the ages, in spite of all the horror and misery that India had gone through. There was poverty and the innumerable progeny of poverty everywhere, and the mark of this beast was on every forehead. This was not pleasant to see, yet that was the basic reality of India. But there was also a mellowness and a gentleness, the cultural heritage of thousands of years, which no amount of misfortune had been able to rub off."

I had recently returned from the South, and during my travels, I had taken several photographs of men, women and children, even though my main mission at the time was to compile a collection of outstanding works of Indian antiquities. Having recently seen a remarkable show of Indian sculpture which the Department of Archaeology had put on in Rashtrapati Bhavan, I was toying with the idea of organizing an exhibition of photographs with a dual theme of combining the life of people in different parts of India with antiquities of the surroundings in which they lived. In harmony with the pictorial tradition of Indian myth and symbol that breaks out like a torrent from among the ruins of the past, its people too appeared to be an integral part of the culture with its intuitive understanding of the anonymous, collective wisdom of India's ageless and multifaceted civilization. My intention was to build a kind of bridge between the traditional customs and legends and the daily reality of life, thus underlining the interaction of Indian art with the common people which transcended temporal experience — bonds that were graphically represented in the man-animal and woman-plant configurations so often seen in Indian art. During this trip, I frequently came across the *Shalabhanjika*, or the configuration in which a woman is shown entwined with a tree: the tradition has it that the dormant procreative forces of nature need to be awakened by a woman through her magic presence. In several parts of India, the *Dohada* rite is still performed in which a virgin is required to embrace a tree in order to inaugurate the harvest season. *Stones that Sing*, I thought, was a suitable title for the proposed exhibition, a metaphorical allusion to this eternal linkage between the people and their art.

Qutub Minar was my point of departure on this long and rewarding journey, during which I visited dozens of historical monuments and archaeological sites. And, indeed, it was a treat to see the subtle relationship between ancient Indian antiquities and the people of a country that traces its civilization back over five thousand years. During my visit to the caves of Ajanta, I was impressed by the validity of Pandit Nehru's observation that seeing a fine type of man or a beautiful woman reminded him of some fresco of ancient times. Looking at the Ajanta paintings, it was as though the people outside the caves were part of the long, never-ending procession of *Jataka* stories painted on the walls of Ajanta. The *Jatakas*, or stories of the Buddha's reincarnation, depicted a vast panorama of landlords and peasants, hunters and fishermen, saints and priests, merchants and shopkeepers, thieves and mendicants, gamblers and dancing girls, and so on. They represented this formidable connection between the people and their art, a relationship which at the same time was interwoven with nature. Passing though numerous hamlets and villages, and visiting tens of temples, mosques, forts and ancient palaces, I saw hardly any separation or barrier between the people and their surroundings. Virtually living in the ruins of ancient monuments, the people were in intimate contact with nature and their animals. There were no boundaries between the villages and the fields and forests, or partitions to separate people from the sacred life-giving rivers and lakes. Even in the tranquillity of the wilderness, there was a teeming flow of life, the fascinating atmosphere that I tried to capture in my photographs.

The freedom movement had provided the emotional content to India's unity in its diversity, and this quality of our life that Pandit Nehru repeatedly emphasized was always present in the back my mind whenever I photographed either people or antiquities. Like their art, people living in different parts of the country had their own characteristics, features and styles: the Punjabis, the Bengalis, the Marathas, the Gujratis, the Andhras, the Oriyas, the Assamese, the Tamils, the Malayalis, the Kashmiris and the Rajputs, had their own peculiar customs and habits. But despite the differences, an incredible unity in diversity existed in India. This mysterious power of cohesion or the "Indian dream of unity", as Pandit Nehru termed it, seemed to draw its enduring vitality from some deep well of broad-based, common culture. In everyday life, it was expressed through ancient epics, legends, myths and festivals, emerging from an undercurrent of common values and approach to life. At one time or another most Hindus, Buddhists, Muslims, Sikhs, Christians, Jains, Parsees and other sects professed different religions, for like people in other parts of the world, Indians often converted to other

Plates 6a and 6b: MILL WORKER'S CHILDREN, TAMIL NADU

faiths. Yet the Indian-ness of common moral and ethical values was never lost, just as foreign influences, particularly through contacts with the Central Asians, the Persians, the Greeks, the Egyptians, the Chinese, the Arabs and the people of the Mediterranean, were selectively absorbed and became a part of an all-embracing Indian culture.

There were no hotels in most of the locations I visited during this trip, and even when there were, as a student I could not afford them. So I stayed in *ashrams* attached to the temples. In the Ranganathan temple at Srirangam, for example, the head priest was kind enough to put me up for two or three days, a sojourn that turned out to be most rewarding, because there I "discovered" an extraordinary statue. My host had ingeniously partitioned off a corner of the gallery in the temple, and converted it into a sort of hut where he lived with his wife and a cow named Parvati. And sitting in its courtyard one morning, I noticed in a corner what appeared to be a part of sculpture that was covered with cakes of cow dung which his wife used for cooking. Curious to find out what was under the muck, I spent several hours removing the heap of garbage piled on it and uncovered, to my utter amazement, a lovely figure of a nude woman (Plate 3). Obviously, poverty and aesthetics could not live together even in a temple embellished with such magnificent art. "A semi-starved nation can have neither religion, nor art, nor organization," stated Mahatma Gandhi in another context. "Whatever can be useful to starving millions is beautiful to my mind. Let us first give them the vital things of life, and only then the graces and ornaments of life will follow."

Nati, as I named her, was a part of an old tradition that is engraved in many a beautiful sculpture of dancing figures seen in south Indian temples. Her controlled turn and poise as well as the sensuality and eloquence of movement effectively reflected the dignity and charm that was and is still the quality of Indian women. Standing in the pose of *tribhanga*, or an inflexion of three bends at the neck, waist and hips, she was cast in the image of local women, several of whom I had photographed working in the fields or standing similarly as they worshipped in the temples. It was as though these female pilgrims had served as models for the sculptor of *Nati*, a phenomenon in which the time gap of so many centuries seemed to have vanished. It was literally what Pandit Nehru once wrote: "If the past had a tendency to become the present, the present also sometimes receded into the distant past and assumed its immobile, statuesque appearance." During the course of my travels, I also shared his sensation that "in the midst of an intensity of action, I was suddenly overcome with a feeling as if

18

it was some past event that I was looking at in retrospect."

During the forties, photographers had to overcome several technical difficulties because at that time cameras were not as sophisticated as today's automatic, computerized machines: it is aptly stated that a camera now does everything for its owner except make a cup of tea. But in those days, it was the man behind the camera who had to do everything from calculating the distance in order to focus on the subject, assessing light conditions before setting the diaphragm, and holding the camera steady as films were not as sensitive as they are now. In this complicated operation, something or the other always went wrong, so that each time "the picture came out", as the significant expression had it, the achievement was no less exciting than a miracle. But what has not changed is the spirit of the man behind the camera, even though in the old days the technical manipulations were infinitely more difficult. Therein lay the difference between my photographs of the people as compared with those of sculptures. For, unlike pictures of antiquities, the portraits of men, women and children were not just illustrations, but living entities with a soul, charged with a poignant human dimension. The interpretation of their moods and emotions called for much more dedication, resourcefulness, innovation, sensitivity and, above all, creativity than mere reproductions of subjects that were static like the antiquities.

Yet there was a subtle interaction between my method of taking photographs of people and of sculptures, a tradition in which it was the human figure that provided the inspiration for Buddhist, Hindu and Jain art. In both cases, the technique I employed was almost the same. I was fascinated by the plastic quality of Indian sculptures in much the same way as I was excited by the sensuality of shapely figures and agile movements of men and women working freely in the open, with no more than a loin-cloth around their waists. I learned from experience that the best time of day to achieve this effect was either early in the morning or late in the afternoon, because side-lighting by the slanting rays of the sun "lifted" the volume of the figures and enhanced the fluidity of swaying curvatures. In this manner, I could translate the plastic quality of bronze and stone into human flesh, and thus achieve the depth of three-dimensional roundness through selectively contrasting light with shadow. Gradually, I then discovered that the *chiaroscuro* effect could be created, not only by manipulating natural lighting on the spot, but also in the darkroom: I found that through blocking certain parts of light from the enlarger lens with either hand or with cardboard cut-outs, some very plain snapshots could be transformed into veritable pictures. Judicious highlighting accentuated the sense of volume and plastic quality, and as in painting, it produced the desired spontaneity of expression I wanted to create in my photographs. It was a sort of key to unlocking the human personality from within, thus making the photographs more responsive to the picturesqueness of the subject. As the images lifted themselves up in the mysteriously dim red light of the darkroom, the thrill of seeing them come to life in different forms and shapes was something like the excitement a sculptor feels when creating solid shapes.

I was not aware at the time that in ancient India the technique of producing relief by shading was called *vartana-karma*. It is described as one of the "eight limbs" of painting methods in an Indian treatise called *Samaranganasutradhara*. In Indian *sastras*, or guides to artistic practice, *citrabhasa*, or painting, could be made "solid" through *ksaya-vriddhi*, or reduction and augmentation of tonal shades. In contrast with the conventional *animnonnata*, or flattened perspective of restricted tonal scale, an image could be *samutthapeti* or "raised up" on a wall surface by means of a brush and colours. Another treatise called *Mahayana Sutralamkara* states: *citre . . . natonnatam nasti cam drsyate atha ca*, which means that "there is no actual relief in pictures, and yet we see it there". Perhaps it was a natural development of ancient Indian practice, when sculptures in the round were gradually flattened out on the railings and walls of Buddhist monuments, and then began to be covered

Plate 7:   CHILDREN PLAYING ON THE BEACH, MALABAR COAST

Plate 8:
A FISHERMAN, KERALA

Plate 9:   FERRY TRANSPORTERS, MALABAR COAST

with layers of bright colours. Thus the rules for painting were equally valid for sculpture; and it was this method of producing a sense of volume and plasticity in my photographs that I erroneously thought was a discovery of my own. Nevertheless, I found the technique to be very effective not only when employed for sculptures but also for producing plastic quality in portrayal of human beings as seen in *A Country Woman* (Plate 11) in Uttar Pradesh; *A Fisherman* (Plate 8) in Kerala; *Two Sisters* (Plate 12) on the Malabar Coast; *A Refugee* (Plate 13) from the Punjab; and several other similar pictures included in this collection.

In the Indian canonical texts, composition was generally described as a combination of *pramanani*, or "rules of proportion" and *sadrshyam*, which means "the correspondence of formal and pictorial elements". Personally, I relied on my own innate sense to frame the composition of the scene on the spot, as well as through balancing the composition by suitably trimming the photographs while enlarging them — the technique known as "cropping". But the surprising part of it was that even my deep-seated impressions of the damaged paintings at Ajanta had imperceptibly crept into my style of painting and photography. As in other spheres of life, in aesthetics as well, some primary experience charged with emotion often creates a permanent impact, which then keeps re-creating itself in different forms. When I saw the Ajanta paintings for the first time, I was greatly dismayed by the destruction they had suffered from time, weather and vandalism. It was not easy to take photographs of whole paintings that were not damaged in one way or another. So unconsciously I seemed to have found a solution by placing the unavoidable damaged patches in positions where, they either did not intrude into the frame of the picture, or helped to improve the composition by counter-balancing some other segment of the painting.

But later I realized to my discomfort that these disconcerting patches on the walls of Ajanta caves had influenced my imagination to such an extent that they began appearing not only in my own paintings, but in my photographic compositions of the people as well. I found that while taking photographs of men, women and children, I had started making use of such undesirable elements as the patches and holes in the ragged clothes of the poor as seen in *Mine Workers* (Plate 61) or *A Refugee Mother* (Plate 28). The damaged wall surfaces that marred Ajanta paintings, and the wretchedness of the poor against which I reacted so strongly seemed to have established a secret alliance with my aesthetic sense, thus enhancing the quality of my paintings and photographs. From this "art for art's sake" point of view, the agile,

24

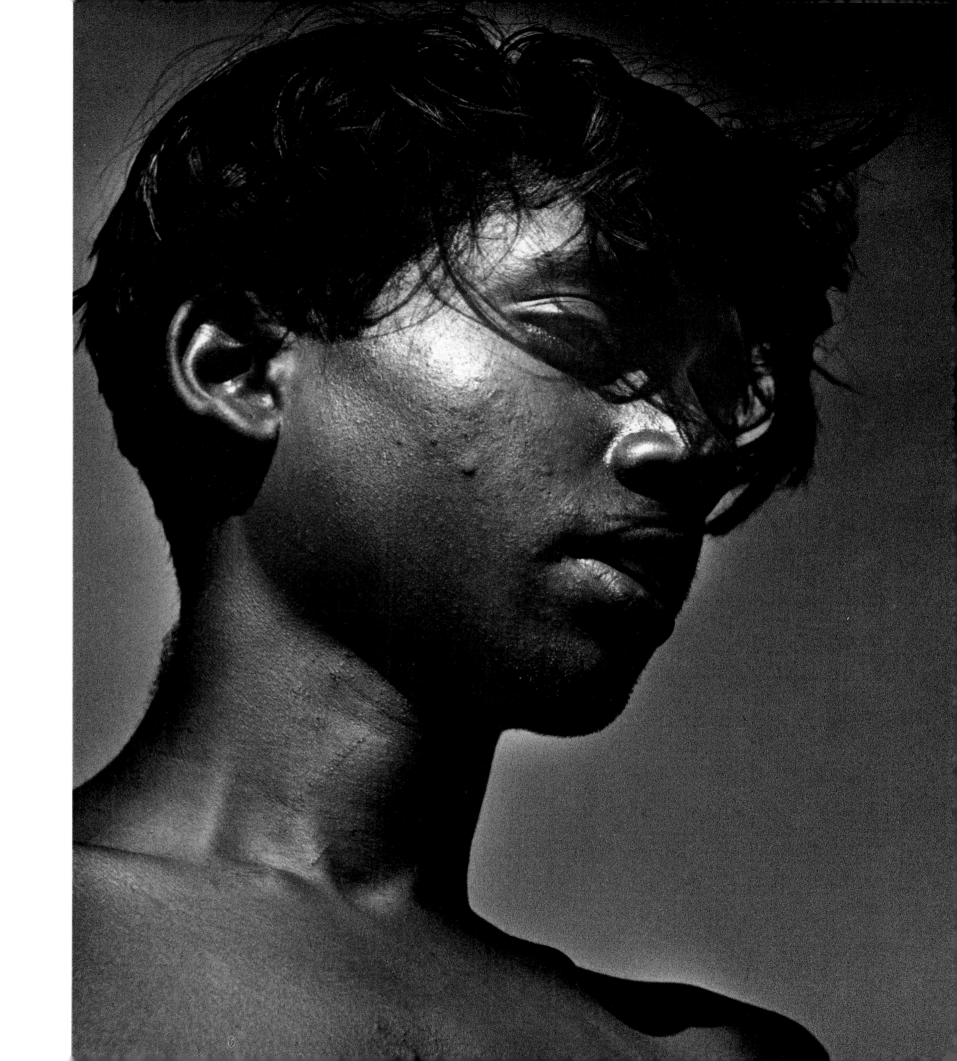

naked bodies of the poor *Mill Worker's Children* (Plates 6a and 6b) with their ebony complexions, appeared to be as fascinating as the plastic sensuality of Pala sculptures in black stone, thus disregarding my revulsion against their miserable condition. It was as though my mind was working at two levels, and my subconscious at the aesthetic level had come round to admitting poverty as a part of reality, the kind of immunity that people develop when exposed to unmitigated misery. Consciously, I abhorred the idea of making a virtue of the ephemeral and the sensational for the sake of novelty, and thus let my aesthetic sensibility overlook the moral outrage I felt against poverty — the art for art's sake attitude that I unequivocally condemned.

The deterioration of the Ajanta paintings was as painful for me as the shambles of heart-wrenching poverty in which the people of the region lived. The paintings seemed to cry out for their urgent restoration in much the same way as the poverty-stricken people clamoured for the improvement in their deplorable existence. Standing before Bodhisattva Padmapani, my spirits were lifted and I felt as though transported into a kind of a magical radiance that was so soothing and relaxing to the senses. At the same time, in the calm and serene face of the Bodhisattva, I saw reflected the sadness and agony on the faces of the poor. It discouraged and demoralized me and its interaction with my sense of social justice was devastating. Art, like nature, was omnipresent in India, but among the people there was none of the joy, enthusiasm and pleasure of living, which in the past had provided the impetus for the development of such magnificent works of art, music, dance and literature. So the twofold theme on which I had set out to build my collection seemed to be turning into its antithesis: the stones did sing and dance as I photographed them on the lovely friezes of South Indian temples, but not the men, women and children who lived right in their midst. Like the hazy atmosphere of the countryside that invariably evoked in me the euphoria of freedom, now unfortunately in my mind the beautiful works of Indian art had become associated with the ugliness of poverty.

Essentially, it was during the Quit India movement that I had effectively come into contact with the people. Many of the prisoners incarcerated with me in Mirzapur jail were workers and peasants who had been arrested in the surrounding villages. At first they were reticent to communicate with persons like me, as our social status seemed to stand in the way. But gradually they had opened up, telling us in bits and pieces their innumerable tales of sor-

row: their crushing and ever-growing burden of rent, illegal exactions, ejectments from land and deprivation of their meagre possessions. Most of them were landless peasants whose small plots of land had been seized, as they could not pay back the huge illegal premiums that the landlords and money-lenders had levied in order to grab their land. Assisted by the police, the landlords preyed on the peasants, like vultures, from all sides. Things did not happen suddenly in their lives for better or for worse. Even their poverty was not of the kind that suddenly destroys; it was the misery of ever-recurring misfortune that trickled agonizingly, drop by drop, from birth to death. Listening to their woes, I felt like Pandit Nehru did when he wrote in *The Discovery of India*: "A new and different India rose up before the young intellectuals who had almost forgotten its existence or attached little importance to it. It was a disturbing sight, not only because of its stark misery and the magnitude of its problems, but because it began to upset some of our values and conclusions. Our reactions varied and depended on our previous environment and experience. Some were already sufficiently acquainted with these village masses; they took them for granted. But for me it was a real voyage of discovery. . ."

One terrible discovery I made during my own trip was at Coimbatore railway station, while I was on my way to my father's estate in the Nilgiris. As the train halted at the station, I saw a poverty-stricken mother with four children, huddled in a corner of the platform. The family was obviously "living" there, as the woman with a tattered sari was lighting a fire in a *chulah* improvised with two bricks, and into it she was shoving all kinds of twigs, old newspapers and other rubbish she had collected. Holding a newly born child in her left arm, she was cooking some kind of southern Indian meal called *sambar* in a discarded canister, as her other three half-naked children looked on with famished eyes, wearing nothing but rags around their waists. Then looking over her shoulders to make sure that no one was watching, the poor woman pulled out of the *chulah* a handful of partly burnt newspaper, and removing its charred edges, she put the pieces of paper in the canister in order to augment the food for her children. Even more incredible was her anxiety to cover up the nakedness and degradation of her poverty, for she did not want anybody to see how she was struggling to survive with her four children in a public place.

My heart began to ache, thinking of how hard and agonizing it must be for that woman to struggle against her stark wretchedness, and yet maintain her human dignity by trying to hide from public view the shame she felt for her poverty. In a different context, it was the sort

Plate 12: TWO SISTERS, MALABAR COAST

of cultural inhibition that had driven thousands of people to starve themselves to a slow and agonizing death during the Bengal famine, rather than eat the cows, which were also starving to death. I abhorred this kind of mentality of self-mortification. I could not understand why these people did not proclaim their plight and discontent loudly at the top of their voices, instead of trying to hide their privations. I hated the sight of people sleeping on the pavements in Calcutta after a hard day's toil as in *A Home in the Street* (Plate 62). Why didn't these people rise up in revolt against such social injustice? Was it not better to die fighting for their rights and live decently, rather than go on lingering in the drudgery of a miserable and hopeless life? Why did they not for once break with the dead past, realize the present and look to the future? It made me angry because in my youthful enthusiasm, I was looking for immediate solutions. I wanted somehow to uproot and discard this kind of death-like immobility that clung to my people so tenaciously. In this regard also I was inspired by Pandit Nehru's ideas, for example his reaction during the Second World War when he wrote: "Vast numbers would die, that was inevitable, but it is better to die fighting than through famine; it is better to die than to live a miserable hopeless life. Out of death, life is born afresh, and individuals and nations who do not know how to die, do not know also how to live. Only where there are graves are there resurrections."

Why did she have four children, when she could not even feed herself, I could not comprehend. After that, I began to notice with even greater concern the hordes of children everywhere, especially among the poor. Whether they were *Children of the Soil* (Plate 16) in the Punjab; *Harijan Children* (Plate 90) in Bombay; or *Coal Miner's Children* (Plate 51) in Bihar, their sheer numbers depressed me, since I learned that over forty per cent of India's population lived below *garibi rekha*, or the poverty line. Yet no facts and figures, however daunting, had given me such a tremendous shock as I felt on seeing the poverty and privations of a mother who was forced to feed her four children on nothing but newspapers. It was this image, more than anything else, that had driven home to me the truth that in countries like India, there was no salvation other than effective family planning and stringent population control with a ceiling on the birth rate no more than zero. I became convinced that curbing excessive population growth and economic development, were the two sides of the same coin, the only currency in which Third World countries could pay to feed the poor and raise their living standard.

ART EXHIBITION AT
LAHORE MUSEUM

***

Photographs and Paintings on Display

PROCEEDS TO HELP RIOT VICTIMS

An exhibition of photographs and oil paintings by Madanjeet was opened in Lahore on Sunday, March 30, at the Punjab University Institute of Chemistry, and will remain open a few more days. The exhibition is organized in aid of the riot sufferers, and a collection was made on the first day when Dr. C. L. Fabri, Curator, Central Museum, opened the show.

Some of the photographs show the shocking and terrible damage done at Amritsar by the rioters; and these prints of smouldering and collapsed houses are deeply moving. Against this savage document of the beastliness of human nature, stand other, happier photographs, eloquent in their emphasis on the beauty of our daily lives in the Punjab: the simplest gateway or the smallest hut can become an object of beauty when seen through the lens of a camera-artist; and the homecoming of the cattle, or ears of corn against the sky, or rows of plants growing in the garden, or again the smiling face of a lovely Punjabi girl silhouetted against the sky, all prove that life could be full of beauty and plenty and happiness, if only we live in peace with each other, without getting at each other's throats.

Madanjeet's paintings are interesting as the experiments of an original mind, though technically he still has to learn a great deal before his oils will be considered as good as his photographs are.

The exhibition is very much worth visiting, and it is hoped that many people will find time in the coming two or three days to go and see this show.

The Civil & Military Gazette: Lahore, 1 April 1947.

Plate 16:
CHILDREN OF THE SOIL,
PUNJAB

My contacts with people in jail had stripped me of many a romantic illusion I had harboured before I jumped into the fray of India's struggle for freedom. There I discovered to my dismay, that the poverty of the peasants and workers apart, their sentiments, too, were radically different from what I imagined. My ideas were essentially the product of the so-called "coffee-house mentality" formed in the Bohemian atmosphere of restaurants where students used to sit for hours, arguing heatedly about what they imagined were the social, economic and political problems of the masses. Our "progressive" ideas about the social status of the poor and how to uplift them in a new order of society, as I found out in prison, were completely flawed. Their concept of freedom and the revolutionary ethos were radically different from the superficial notions held by people like me who came from the upper strata of society. No argument made any sense to them unless explained in terms of their land, their animals and their meagre necessities for survival. It was poverty that moulded their behaviour as they patiently ploughed the tough furrows of endless toil. Literally down-to-earth, they were not in the least interested in our intellectual exercises or the theoretical nuances that could not directly explain in practical terms the simplest way to improve their lot. Poverty was the master not only of thought but of style as well, a truth about which I was ignorant when I was a student at Benares Hindu University.

During the forties, the student community in Benares was sharply divided into two groups, one supporting Pandit Nehru and the other owing its allegiance to Mahatma Gandhi, as if the two leaders were working against each other. I was a prominent member of the Nehru group, and staunchly opposed the orthodoxy of Gandhian ideas. Nehru was my apostle, and I tried to cast myself in the image of my revolutionary hero and viewed everything through his modern vision of a secular, industrialized, prosperous and socialist India. I deplored the protagonists of Mahatma Gandhi as "backward traditionalists" who wanted to drag the country into the pristine *status quo* of an Indian village. Was not Mahatma Gandhi's concern for the untouchables a mere whitewash? I would argue. Had he ever openly denounced the *chaturvarna ashram* system of the Hindu social order? On the contrary, I would assert, he had publicly expressed the view that the four-*varna* system still had a useful function to perform in Indian society. It clearly proved, I thought, that Mahatma Gandhi himself believed in the theory of separation and purity of the four castes with the *brahmins* at the top and the *sudras* at the bottom. I compared him unfavourably with such social reformers as Raja

Plate 18: SIKH PEASANTS GOING TO THE POLLS, PUNJAB

Plate 19: A VILLAGE SCENE, PUNJAB

Plate 20: TIME FOR REJOICING, PUNJAB

Plate 21: AFTER A HARD DAY'S WORK, PUNJAB

Ram Mohan Roy who, I believed, fought much more courageously to rid India of the traditional savageries such as *sati* and other degrading post-Vedic superstitions, than the Mahatma was prepared to do.

I hated the mentality of discrimination which, I knew, was deeply rooted in the Indian psyche since the Aryans, the "pure ones", migrated into the Indian subcontinent and established a social system that classified people in different castes. It was a manifestation of this racial attitude that appeared daily in Indian newspaper advertisements, seeking fair-skinned brides and bridegrooms, and for the same reason, I detested those who were against intercommunity marriages. Clearly, it was a refined form of apartheid that specified who cooked your food; with whom you could eat; whom you could marry; how marriages should be performed by different castes; what kind of clothes and ornaments a woman must wear; and even such ludicrous things as whether or not a man could carry an umbrella. Caste divided the labour market; the *sudras* or the untouchables were only fit to become scavengers, and forced to do dirty work at low wages. I wanted to see the hierarchy of social discrimination abolished in *all* sections of society, and not as it affected only the *harijans*, or the "sons of God", as Mahatma Gandhi euphemistically called the untouchables. The Indian variety of apartheid, I thought, was much more difficult to combat than the black apartheid against which Mahatma Gandhi had fought so bravely in South Africa, because here the struggle against racial discrimination was not just against a white-skinned government, but a thick-skinned mentality that was even more difficult to root out because it was deeply entrenched over a period of some three thousand years.

Barring the *harijans* from entering Hindu temples was not just a religious or social stigma. It was inextricably interwoven with the economic hegemony of the upper castes, and the exploitation of the deprived sections of society. Until I went to prison, I was not aware of the cold-blooded murders, brutalities and discriminations to which the *harijans* and *adivasi* were subjected, especially in some of the districts in Bengal, Bihar, and Orissa: *adivasi* were the so-called primitive tribes such as the Mundas, Santhals, Kurmi Mahatos. With me in jail was a student leader of the Jharkhand movement, representing the tribal forest-dwellers, and he was the one who first revealed to me some of the incredible atrocities and humiliations to which these helpless people were subjected by the local landlords belonging to higher castes. He told me of forced migrations; chain-gangs in mines and factories doing low-paid hazardous work;

Plate 23:
PORTRAIT OF A MUSLIM
PEASANT, PUNJAB

ejections from land; bonded or semi-slave agricultural labourers; and the uprooting of peasants from their hearths and homes to provide cheap labour in plantations and industries outside the region. These unfortunate people dared not even protest, and those who raised their voices suffered terrible retribution. I could not bear hearing the hair-raising stories of how the hired hoodlums of money-lenders, landgrabbers and local tyrants massacred whole families of *harijans* and *adivasis,* raping their women, and bludgeoning their children to death. It was then that I came to realize how superficial and irrelevant our knowledge was of what was happening in many parts of India, and the reason why Pandit Nehru had associated B.R. Ambedkar, the leader of the untouchables, with the framing of the constitution of independent India. I had taken several photographs of people who were later called the scheduled castes, as seen in *A Harijan Family* (Plate 52) in Bombay; and also of the tribals who were classified as scheduled tribes such as *Toda Tribesmen* (Plate 53), whom I had photographed in the Nilgiris.

The socio-political ferment among the student community in Lahore, on the other hand, had a different complexion. Against the background of a comparatively richer peasantry in the Punjab, here the emphasis was more on the social rather than economic aspects of political life. The movement was supported by several left-wing intellectuals such as Gurbaksh Singh and Faiz Ahmed Faiz, the eminent poet. For the first time, young people had mustered the courage to defy their elders, questioning the morality and other components of the social structure, and challenging both the religious and cultural validity of the age-old establishment. It was essentially a revolt against antiquated and austere Islamic customs, which over the years had become integrated into Hindu and Sikh culture as well. Freudian ideas had caught hold of the imagination of the youth, as these notions were considered to be in tune with those of Marxism. Against the background of society's iron-clad framework of strict taboos, the passion for free-wheeling individualism of the forties in Lahore was much more radical than the Western non-conformism of the sixties because, in addition, it was coupled with the freedom movement. And as generally happens in such situations, perhaps it was the main reason why the reaction of Muslim fundamentalism was so severe because these progressive ideas were the antithesis of its outmoded social rigidity. Such writers and poets were greatly admired by young people like me with radical ideas, and inspired by these ideals, I had taken a number of photographs of the working class in Lahore such as *Portrait of a Railway Worker* (Plate 17).

Politically, my reservations about Mahatma Gandhi had already mollified during the Quit India movement when against his will, he had agreed to Congress participation in the war if India could function as a free country. As Pandit Nehru pointed out: "For him this was a remarkable and astonishing change, involving suffering of the mind and pain of the spirit — the practical statesman took precedence over the uncompromising prophet." But it was not until the breathtaking role Mahatma Gandhi played in order to stop the horrible communal carnage between Hindus and Muslims that my respect for him blossomed into unmitigated admiration. Following the failure of the British Government mission led by Lord Pethick-Lawrence and Sir Stafford Cripps, the distant rumbling of the approaching storm could already be heard during the summer of 1946. The ominous foreboding had become loud and clear with the menacing proclamation of Direct Action Day by the Muslim League, resulting in what came to be known as the Great Calcutta Killing in which about 4,000 innocent people lost their lives. I was amazed by the courageous manner in which Mahatma Gandhi, disregarding his own personal safety, walked barefoot through the riot-torn villages of Bengal and Bihar on his peace mission. He spent several months living among Muslims in Noakhali, and was condemned by religious partisans of both communities. Yet he clung to his moral principles, admonishing the bigots, consoling the victims and at the same time trying to help in rehabilitation of the refugees. It was an incredible spectacle, one reason why Albert Einstein was prompted to state: "Generations to come would scarce believe that such a one as this ever in flesh and blood walked upon this earth."

Notwithstanding Mahatma Gandhi's heroic effforts, the bloodthirsty communal monster had then moved out of Bengal, destroying and setting afire thousands of peace-loving homes in the small towns and villages of Assam, Bihar and the United Provinces and, at the beginning of March 1947, its bloody claws began to tear apart the communal amity in the Punjab. I clearly remember 4 March, the day when the conflagration began, because I myself was a witness to the spark that set it aflame. My final exams were only two months away, and as I sat studying in my dormitory of the New Hostel, I heard a commotion outside. Peeping through the window, I saw a student leader addressing a group of people who had gathered in the square in front of Government College. Suddenly, the police appeared out of nowhere and started shooting at random into the crowd, killing and wounding a number of people. Serious rioting broke out immediately, and spread throughout the city. The situation became

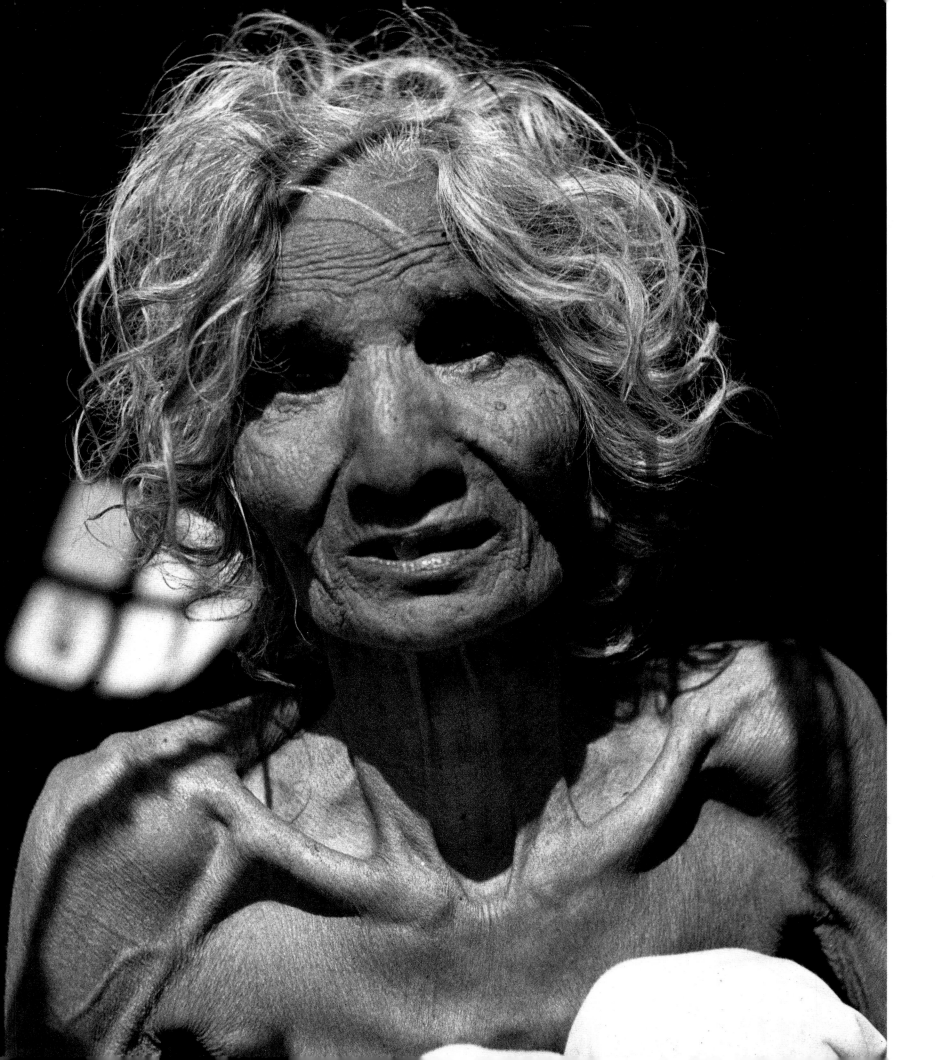

worse in the following days as the killings and burning of houses and looting of shops intensified. Innocent pedestrians were indiscriminately stabbed in the streets, and hospitals could no longer accommodate the increasing number of people who were brought in for emergency medical treatment. Significantly, the first dust storms of the summer prematurely hit the city, a memory which in my mind became identified with the horror of rioting: since childhood, dust storms in Lahore terrified me, as in the hot oppressive quietness before the impending storm, I would see the pitch-black darkness of a brown mountain of dust rise in the sky, and then descend to envelop us with a blinding fury in which I used to suffer unbearable claustrophobia.

Schools and colleges having closed, there was an eerie atmosphere of calm before the storm as the streets of Lahore become completely deserted. A general exodus of students emptied my boarding house as well, and without any servants, the hostel mess was shut down. For me, it was impossible to reach my parents who lived far south in the Nilgiri hills where my father, Dogar Singh, had settled down on a tea-estate after he retired from the Travancore State service. He had started his career as a professor at the Hindu University, and that was why I had continued my studies at Benares until the authorities expelled me from the United Provinces after my release from prison. For ideological reasons, I never felt comfortable in my grandfather Makhan Singh's palatial joint family house in Lahore cantonment. Because of his obsequious background, the colonial masters had decorated him with the title of Sardar Bahadur; and during my childhood he had once severely punished me for singing a popular ballad about Sukhdev, Bhagat Singh and Rajguru, the three Indian patriots who had been hanged. Instead, I decided to spend a few days in Preet Nagar as I also wanted to consult Gurbaksh Singh and seek his advice about my future course of action. In that period of crisis, when the very texture of society was being torn asunder, and many a stalwart of secularism had succumbed, Gurbaksh Singh had doggedly continued propagating the message of communal harmony through *Preet Lari.*

Unfortunately, I could not go to Preet Nagar directly, as the bus services had been suspended because of the rioting. So I took a train to Amritsar in the hope that from there I might be able to find some transport to the colony that lay about half-way between Lahore and Amritsar. And as I reached the station, I saw another train from Batala coming to a halt on the other side of the platform. To my horror, I saw that blood was dripping from the crevices under

Plate 27:
A REFUGEE MOTHER
AND CHILD, PUNJAB

Plate 28:
A REFUGEE MOTHER,
PUNJAB

the doors of the compartments which were full of dead and wounded passengers. A mob at Sharifpura, a suburb of Amritsar, had intercepted the train and had attacked the passengers with knives, hatchets and stones. It is impossible to describe the traumatic experience. After all these years, I still feel the horror of the gruesome sight of hundreds of passengers mercilessly butchered. Men, women and children lay dead with heads almost severed, arms and legs chopped off, bellies ripped open, intestines protruding, eyes plucked out. In a women's compartment, a naked woman lay with her breast torn off, her one hand still gripping the door handle in an attempt to escape. I was so petrified that my senses stopped functioning, and a buzzing noise in my head drowned out the wails and screams of the terror-stricken men, women and children as they scrambled and rushed out of the bloody compartments of the train.

"You must be mad even to think of putting on a show in conditions such as these," a friend of mine remarked when he learned that I was planning a peace exhibition of my photographs and paintings. Indeed he was right, because it was a very dangerous period when we were virtually sitting on the top of a land-mine about to explode. Lord Louis Mountbatten had just arrived to become the new Viceroy of India, and he announced that the goal of a united India was no longer feasible. In the Punjab, the Unionist ministry had resigned, and no party could contain the rising tide of hatred that was welling up between Muslims, Hindus and Sikhs. In an atmosphere charged with suspicion and hatred when passions were running high, the task was not only difficult, but extremely risky. Yet I decided to go ahead and organize a peace exhibition, inspired as I was by the manner in which Mahatma Gandhi had thrown himself heart and soul into the task of healing the scars of communal conflict. My conscience could not ignore what I had seen with my own eyes in Amritsar. I wanted somehow to expose the perfidy and the callous ambitions of the communal leaders who were deliberately misleading innocent people in the name of religion and inciting them to commit the most atrocious crimes.

Not so long before, I had witnessed a heart-warming spectacle of communal unity at Lahore railway station, when a huge mass of people, representing all communities, had given a heroic welcome to three army officers — a Hindu, a Muslim and a Sikh. The officers had been imprisoned by the British for having joined the Indian National Army which some exiles had formed in Japanese-occupied territories during the war. And after a public trial at the Red Fort

PUNJAB YESTERDAY AND TODAY

***

Photographic Exhibition

_____

BY A STAFF REPORTER

Mr. Madanjeet's exhibition of photographs, is an example of what a camera properly handled can do in the hands of an artist.

The main purpose behind the exhibition which, contrary to so many we have had, shows careful planning, was to present pictorially life in the Punjab as it used to be before it became the scene of communal strife, and as it is today. No more effective indictment of violence could have been presented to the public.

Each of the seven sections into which the photographs are grouped, portrays a phase of that life. The exhibits are of a high standard, particularly *Our Workers* which is a study in expressions, and *The Cold Blooded Murder*, an inspiring if all too horrible a picture of the riots.

To many the photographer's pictures are familiar as some of them have been reproduced in a number of journals and periodicals. Judging from the technique of his work, it is difficult to imagine that these photographs were made with economy of material and lack of proper equipment, some even with a borrowed camera.

Himself a refugee from Lahore, Mr. Madanjeet is donating the proceeds of the sales to a relief fund for refugees. The exhibition organized by the All-India Fine Arts and Crafts Society, will remain open daily from 2 to 7 p.m. up to November 12.

Times of India: New Delhi, 3 November 1947

Plate 30: SUNSET AT A VILLAGE, PUNJAB

in New Delhi, they had just been released because of political intervention by Mahatma Gandhi and Pandit Nehru. During the trial that lasted for several months, I was among the student demonstrators who joined a huge procession through the streets of Lahore. I had also met Maulana Abul Kalam Azad, the Congress President, on his arrival in the Punjab in connection with the formation of the Ministry following the 1946 General Elections. The tumultuous reception and the rapturous display of communal unity with which the people of Lahore had welcomed the INA officers, were so overwhelming that I was at a loss to comprehend how the same people could become so insane as to carry out such brutalities against each other. Thus, by contrasting the pictures I had taken during happier times, with the recent images of death and destruction recorded in Lahore and particularly in Amritsar, I wanted to re-create the marvellous atmosphere that the INA trio symbolized. By comparing the fearful darkness of fratricidal conflict with the contented, healthy aspects of life I had photographed in the sunshine of rural Punjab, my aim was to reveal the ugly face of communal strife and highlight the virtues of communal harmony.

Among the photographs I had taken in the Punjab villages during happier times were some striking portraits of sturdy peasants — Muslims, Hindus and Sikhs — living peacefully and working in co-operation with each other. Among them were people with happy contented faces, strong characters and sincere souls as in the *Portrait of a Muslim Peasant* (Plate 23). Especially in the villages around Preet Nagar, I had witnessed some very inspiring scenes during the General Elections and taken dozens of photographs of Sikh peasants who had flocked to vote for the secular ideals of the Congress as recorded in *Sikh Peasants Going to the Polls* (Plate 18). Travelling through the lovely fertile countryside, I had photographed people belonging to all communities as they worked together in the fields, or in their moments of relaxation, sat in groups around the *hukka,* as seen in *Time of Rejoicing* (Plate 20) and *After a Hard Day's Work* (Plate 21). In the Punjab villages, the *hukka,* or water-pipe, was symbolic of social amity, and the greatest punishment for a culprit was to deprive him of his *hukka-pani,* or pipe and water. One striking picture of village cordiality was *The Consultation* (Plate 22) as I had seen a Muslim peasant so engrossed in deep conversation with his Hindu friend, that they did not even notice that someone was taking their photograph. I had also made a number of pictures of some Punjabi women, one of which was *A Milkmaid* (Plate 15).

I was fortunate to have at my disposal a well-equipped photographic darkroom at the

Institute of Chemistry, my alma mater. For some time I had been experimenting with photographic emulsions, and had in fact succeeded in making a prototype paper of my own with a beautiful rough texture, on which the image appeared to be hand-made. My idea at the time was eventually to put on a show of photographs printed on my own paper. The rioting not only destroyed that ambition, but I could not even buy any kind of photographic paper as the market was closed. So if it had not been for the kindness of the Director who allowed me to use the paper in store at the Institute, my exhibition would never have seen the light of day. In a race against time, I quickly selected a set of negatives and started making enlargements at all hours of the day and night, as I wanted to overtake the fast-moving events. I worked even harder when I learned from the news media that Pandit Nehru was himself expected to visit Lahore during the middle of March, and I toyed with the wild idea of persuading him to open the show. Apart from my cherished dream of meeting Pandit Nehru in person, I was anxious to attract public attention and thus promote the cause that I knew was very dear to the Congress leader as well. Unfortunately, my hopes were thwarted, and the disappointment I felt was great even if the very thought of approaching Panditji was no more than a flight of my own imagination. Nevertheless, the deadline I had thus set in expectation of Pandit Nehru's arrival did spur me on to mount the exhibition within the record time of a fortnight.

The photographs of arson, death and destruction exhibited in Lahore were mostly taken at Amritsar, the town where I was stranded for two days during my abortive trip to Preet Nagar. And judging from the reviews that appeared in local newspapers, I had apparently succeeded in what I wanted to convey. "Some of the photographs show the shocking and terrible damage done at Amritsar by the rioters," commented a staff reporter of *The Civil & Military Gazette* on 1 April 1947, "and these prints of smouldering and collapsed houses are deeply moving. Against this savage document of the beastliness of human nature, stand other happier photographs, eloquent in their emphasis on the beauty of our daily lives in the Punjab: the simplest gateway or the smallest hut can become an object of beauty when seen through the lens of a camera artist; and the home-coming of the cattle, or ears of corn against the sky, or rows of plants growing in a garden, or again a smiling face of a lovely Punjabi girl silhouetted against the sky, all prove that life could be full of beauty and plenty and happiness, if only we live in peace with each other, without getting at each other's throats."

The Tribune, another important Lahore daily, also lauded my effort, and even though

I was happy with the reviews, in my heart I knew that I had failed to evoke the public response I expected to generate. In the vicious communal atmosphere then prevailing in Lahore, nobody was really interested in a show of this kind, much less in the message I was trying to put across. In fact several important political leaders, both Hindu and Muslim, had declined my request to open the exhibition as they were either afraid of its political implications or did not want to risk their lives. In the end, the show was inaugurated by a foreigner, Dr C.L.Fabri, who was at that time the Curator of Central Museum in Lahore. Principal C.H. Rice of the Forman Christian College was the only other prominent person present, and significantly he was also a non-Indian. Others who came for the opening were mostly my classmates and some student leaders representing the Students' Federation. On the whole, it was a lone cry in the wilderness, a personal success but a public failure. Nevertheless, when the British Cabinet Mission published its scheme during the following month and both the Congress and the Muslim League accepted it in principle, I was delighted by the course of events. Once again I became optimistic that India's communal difficulties could be settled through negotiations and that the country would not be partitioned. Unfortunately, it was the last splutter of a dying candle and these hopes were dashed as quickly as they had emerged.

The horrendous events that followed soon after the Mountbatten partition plan was announced in June 1947, are now a part of history. They were so shocking that, as I fled Lahore, for several months I remained in a dazed state, the so-called post-traumatic stress disorder. It was the kind of amnesia I had once experienced after a car accident when I could not recall the mishap, nor feel the injuries. In the aftermath of partition, about eight million people were hounded from their hearths and homes, leaving behind all they possessed in Pakistan, and about the same number made the nightmare journey in the opposite direction. And as they fled for their lives, over 200,000 men, women and children were brutally butchered in a communal carnage of hysterical mass savagery. Most probably my story might have also ended at this juncture, had it not been for the kindness of a *tonga* coachman in Lahore, who saved my life as he was driving me to the railway station. The incident is worth narrating because, as described in my book, *The White Horse,* it shows how in the midst of the dark bewilderment of communal insanity, a solitary act of compassion by a humble individual restored and rejuvenated my faith in the inherent goodness of my people, and boosted my spirits when they had hit rock bottom.

Plate 33: A PEOPLE'S POET, KASHMIR

Plate 34: CHILDREN PLAYING PEOPLE'S MILITIA, KASHMIR

Plate 35: A STUDENT ACTRESS, KASHMIR

ABDULLAH OPENS
EXHIBITION OF PHOTOGRAPHS

***

BY A STAFF REPORTER

Opening an exhibition of photographs by Mr. Madanjeet at Exhibition Hall, New Delhi, on Wednesday, Sheikh Abdullah, premier of Jammu and Kashmir, said that the artist was one who, out of love of the Kashmiris, had come to help build up the Kashmir Cultural Front last year.

About a hundred photographs, neatly arranged and excellently presented, gave an accurate impression of Kashmir's struggle against the tribal invaders from Pakistan. Mr. Madanjeet has taken great pains to combine the artistic with the topical. Each photograph is, in fact, a story by itself.

Mr. Madanjeet is a great exponent of the light and shadow technique. His effects are essentially created by contrast. One of the best of India's photographers, his work is already known in Delhi.

The Hindustan Times: New Delhi, 20 August 1948.

Plate 36: A VIEW FROM THIKSE MONASTERY, LADAKH

Plate 37: CHILDREN FISHING IN A LAKE, KASHMIR

Plate 38: GIRL IN A *SHIKARA*, KASHMIR

On the day of my bid to escape from Lahore, all the Hindu and Sikh taxi-drivers had fled or were in hiding, and so it was impossible to find any transport to the railway station. Leaving behind all my baggage, I started walking towards the main street with only a hand-bag. It was a very hot day, and the few trees along the road provided hardly any shade. I frequently looked over my shoulder, fearing that someone might be following me because in most cases of stabbing, the cowardly hooligans usually attacked their victims from behind. Tired and perspiring profusely from the heat and the tension building up inside me, I finally reached the main road and stood beneath a tree: I was afraid to take a taxi or a *tonga*, not knowing who the driver might be because lately some of them had attacked their clients. Time was running out, and I could not wait any longer lest I missed the train. So I was left with little option but to stop the first *tonga* coming in my direction. I regarded the driver with a great deal of misgiving and even though I knew that the hefty, bearded coachman was a Muslim, I requested him to drive me to the railway station.

The *tonga* started moving, and there was a long period of oppressive silence in which I could not tell which was the louder, my heartbeats or the trot of the horse. Unable to see the *tongawalla*'s face I wondered what the devil was going on in his head. I tried talking to him, telling him about the merits of communal harmony, but failed to evoke any response. By this time the *tonga* was passing through a narrow street, and my heart sank to see directly in front a mob armed with knives and hatchets, throwing stones and looting a shop. This was the end, I thought, because with my turban and the prevailing anger against the Sikhs, I could not possibly escape the mob's frenzy. The coachman pulled back the reins and stopped. My first reaction was to jump and flee, but that would have been reckless and futile in that predominantly Muslim locality. I was trapped and completely at the mercy of the coachman. He turned back and looked at me like a judge who was about to pronounce his verdict of life or death. I looked back with pleading eyes, and holding my breath, waited in silence. Then to my astonishment, he whispered, "Stoop low!" and shouting a mouthful of Punjabi swear-words, he whipped the horse hard. The *tonga* gathered speed as I ducked behind the wooden partition of the seat, and before the mob realized who I was, the vehicle barged through the gang of hooligans. The tremendous power of this silent, solitary act of compassion on the part of an ordinary *tongawalla* in Lahore was like a ray of light in that terrifying darkness, and greatly helped to boost my spirits. Perhaps it was nature's gift for the spiritual survival of mankind

in periods of crisis in order to outlive millions of evil deeds.

The political *volte-face* was so violent that I was completely confused and demoralized when I reached New Delhi. Until the end of March, Mahatma Gandhi was adamantly against partition. "If the Congress wishes to accept partition, it will be over my dead body," he had stated on his return from Noakhali. Like most Hindu and Sikh refugees from the Punjab and Muslims in India, I felt betrayed because I could not comprehend what kind of "political realism" it was that compelled the Congress leadership to accept the Mountbatten plan. Acquiescence to partition on the basis of religion was the antithesis of all the secular principles of Indian cultural unity, as it was shortsighted not to foresee the effect of its implications on other religious communities in the subcontinent. Involuntarily carried along on a formidable crest of a political wave, I was flung ashore into a shattered country where I felt lost and impotent. And as though in an effort to to retrieve some of the scattered pieces of my disintegrating idealism, I volunteered to join the *Diwan Hall Refugee Camp* (Plate 25) which had just been established in order to assist the helpless refugees, some of whom had already started arriving in Delhi.

The camp was no more than a few hurriedly improvised tents that had been pitched facing the historic Red Fort on the opposite side of the main road that connects New Delhi with the old part of the city. It hardly sufficed to shelter the innumerable refugees as men, women and children were crammed together in filthy conditions, cooking and sleeping mostly in the open. Scared of the uncertain future, these miserable people in their rags and tatters looked like hunted animals. Their wretchedness, suffering and desperation was difficult to bear as I heard the distressing cries of the orphans, sighs of the widows, and groans of the aged and the wounded. It was veritable hell to witness the several agonizing deaths of old people, women giving birth without any assistance; and in one case the terrible suicide of a woman, who had left a note on her body, yearning for the home she had to abandon in Lahore and grieving for her family, all of whom had been killed.

Most of the camp's inmates were women, as their men had either been killed or were trudging from door to door in search of work. It was heartbreaking to listen to their unending tales of woe. But what I found even more touching was the sad, distant look in their eyes that expressed agony far beyond words. The silent gaze that stared beyond eternity epitomized all the sufferings of their ordeal and poignantly expressed feelings that seemed to emerge from the deep unconscious. Until then I was under the impression that as in painting, my photographs too could depict a variety of emotions like love, hate, anger, compassion, happiness and grief by characteristic facial expressions, and eyes were just one component of it. But now I discovered that the eyes in themselves were the mirror of the soul, especially when the intensity of feeling crossed the threshold of the unbearable. There was something mysterious in those eyes that established a silent, sympathetic bond with my own emotions and notwithstanding the almost four decades that have since elapsed, I still feel the same painful sensation in that haunting look of the eyes as when these photographs were taken. They still produce in my limbs the kind of numb, cold insensibility that I experienced when I had been a horrified witness of the train massacre at Amritsar.

Perhaps it was a good illustration of how archetypal images appear in actual life: they are at the same time both images and emotions, interacting simultaneously. The image in itself was of course important, but when charged with emotion, it acquired a psychic energy or "numinosity" that was dynamic and transcendental. Carl Gustav Jung had derived this notion from the ancient doctrine of *signatura rerum*, the sign of things, a theory that was employed and enlarged by Agrippa of Nettesheim and also by Paracelsus. According to this doctrine, things have a hidden meaning that is expressed in their external form, inasmuch as this form points to another, not directly visible, level of reality. It was not just an image but a phenomenon of human dimensions that I saw in the hopeless eyes of *A Refugee Widow* (Plate 29), who had lost everything she owned in this world. The poignancy of her desperation was as intense as the dazed stare of distress of *A Refugee Grandmother* (Plate 26), even though her eyes were foggy: the old woman died the day after this photograph was taken. The distant look in the eyes of *A Refugee Mother and Child* (Plate 27), seemed to unfold the entire history of that period of torment, of the unbearable vicissitudes of millions of men, women and children who were violently uprooted, of their helplessness and despair.

On the eve of Independence, I was held up in the camp to assist a woman during childbirth because no doctors or nurses were available. From the camp, I could see tremendous excitement around the Red Fort across the road, as masses of people had already started gathering even though the flag-hoisting ceremony was not until the following day. By virtue of my being a volunteer at the refugee camp, I had managed to obtain a pass for the special midnight ceremony at the Constituent Assembly, and I was eagerly looking forward to attending

74

Plate 42: A CHILD ARTISAN, KASHMIR

Plate 43: A CHILD EMBROIDERER, KASHMIR

Plate 44:
GOATHERD BATHING
HIS ANIMAL, KASHMIR

Plate 45: A PEASANT FAMILY, KASHMIR

Plate 46:
PORTRAIT OF A PEASANT,
KASHMIR

Plate 47: PEASANT WITH GRANDSON, KASHMIR

the inauguration of India's freedom. Pacing up and down impatiently, I waited outside the tent in which the woman was in labour, praying for the early birth of the baby, thus making it possible for me to keep my appointment. I recall how terribly nervous I felt, not knowing what to do in a situation like this as I did not know anything about childbirth. And finally when I heard the cries of the newly born infant and entered the tent, I was shocked to see in the dim light of a smoking kerosene lantern that in the meantime the child had died and the mother was holding the corpse with both her hands. Depressed by the infant's death, and extremely exhausted from the day's work, I no longer felt like going to the Parliament House. Instead, I got on my bicycle and pedalled wearily back to Daryaganj where I used to sleep in a tiny two-room apartment along with the numerous relations of my three uncles from Lahore, who had also taken refuge in New Delhi.

Being young, I was able to endure many a hardship, but my mother's three elder brothers and their families found their exile extremely difficult to bear. Born and bred in the luxury of their father's wealth in Lahore, it was as much a torment for them to live in a dilapidated apartment in a filthy locality of Faiz Bazar as it was repellent to work in an improvised motor garage across the road where they were obliged to make ends meet. On top of it all, they had to put up with relatives like me who had nowhere else to go. Everyone was asleep as I entered the apartment, and I dropped into bed, still wearing my shoes as I did not have enough strength even to change my clothes. But I could not sleep, wondering about what was going on in the main hall of the Constituent Assembly. Not wanting to wake up the others who were sleeping in the same room, I pressed the portable radio close to my ear and, lowering its volume to a minimum, switched it on. Pandit Nehru had already started speaking, and the first thing I heard was his familiar voice: "Long years ago, we made a tryst with destiny and now the time comes when we shall redeem our pledge. At the stroke of the midnight hour, when the world sleeps, India will wake to life and freedom. A moment comes, which comes but rarely in history, when we step out of the old to the new, when an age ends and when the soul of a nation, long suppressed, finds utterance. It is fitting that at this solemn moment we take the pledge of dedication to the service of India and her people, and to the still larger cause of humanity."

The speech produced a bizarre effect on me — tears welled up in my eyes, rolled down my cheeks and I began to weep in the quietness of my solitude. It was as though a mighty dam

of suppressed emotions had suddenly burst, unleashing a flood of feelings that were a strange mixture of both joy and pain, of torment and excitement. Mauled by the horrible ordeal of communal carnage that had literally torn my country apart, the dawn of freedom in a divided India was certainly not as I had dreamt it would be. The feeling was a strange blend of regret and relief. It was as though in the midst of the havoc caused by floods, I heard the melodious gurgle of a mountain stream, or as if in the midst of forest fires, I sensed the warmth of a fluttering flame in a homely hearth. I missed the wonderful college days I had spent in Lahore and at the same time felt intense revulsion against the holocaust that followed. With one ear I heard the inspiring poetry of Faiz, and with the other the fundamentalist harangues of the religious bigots. And now in New Delhi, I heard the trumpet of freedom jarred by the wails of the woman whose baby had just died in the squalor of the refugee camp in which I was obliged to work. My *Tale of Two Cities* was no different from that of Charles Dickens as I recalled his famous lines: "It was the best of times. It was the worst of times."

After the disappointing reaction in Lahore to the message I was trying to convey through my photographs and paintings, I might not have organized another peace exhibition in New Delhi, had not rioting also flared up in the capital. Until the first week of September 1947, the simmering communal discontent in Delhi was kept under control, mainly because the news media had wisely refrained from reporting the terrible happenings in the Punjab. But as more and more refugees arrived and began narrating their gruesome stories of horror, the hysteria of collective communal insanity overpowered Delhi as well. It started with the killing of some workers, and the awful fire of revenge in the hearts of the refugees then spread like a bush-fire, resulting in large-scale slaughter, looting and the burning of property. Particularly in Connaught Place, New Delhi's main market, the miscreants were very active, looting and occupying shops and properties vacated by their Muslim owners as they fled for their lives. It was a repeat performance of the terrible scenes I had witnessed in Lahore and Amritsar, but with the difference that now under the leadership of Mahatma Gandhi and Pandit Nehru, the communal fanatics were on the defensive.

A fantastic scene in which I myself saw Pandit Nehru personally chasing a hooligan in Connaught Place, has remained engraved in my memory as a shining example of the lofty ideals that inspired this great leader. I was just coming out of a photographer's studio where I had gone to collect some photographs taken in the refugee camp, when suddenly I had a glimpse of Panditji passing by the inner circle of the market. And as I rushed out to take a closer look, I was astonished to see him leaping out of the car which was still moving, and chasing a group of miscreants who were trying to break open a shop. There was great commotion as the security men jumped from their motorcycles and ran after the Prime Minister, trying to protect him. I ran in that direction as well, and saw how furious he was, protesting loudly and trying to break out of the cordon which the security men had formed around him. Waving a baton in the air, his face was red with rage as he returned to the car, audibly cursing. It was a marvellous spectacle that gladdened my heart, releasing deep-seated emotions that were troubling my soul. During that month, Mahatma Gandhi, too, achieved a spectacular triumph when his fasting succeeded in stopping the rioting in Calcutta. Somehow I felt as though I had been personally vindicated

These events encouraged me to try once more to propagate the message of communal harmony through an exhibition of my pictures, the way I had attempted in Lahore. But it was not easy because here I did not have the facilities I enjoyed at the Institute of Chemistry in Lahore. I did not even possess a good camera, having abandoned most of my photographic equipment in Lahore, when I had fled for my life. Even if I had the means to buy the required equipment, I could not possibly assemble it immediately, as events were now racing ahead with an even greater speed than in Lahore. So I thought of approaching the proprietor of Photo Service Company — the studio where I had just seen Panditji — and requested him to let me use his darkroom for this purpose. To my pleasant surprise, Babuji, the owner of the studio, not only agreed to let me do so free of charge, but on his own lent me a better camera. He even went to the extent of letting me use his darkroom after the closing hours, because during the day I was busy working in the refugee camp. On such occasions, he entrusted me with the keys of his studio, and collected them the next morning when he came to open the shop. Thus I began organizing another exhibition and, as in Lahore, sometimes worked for whole nights. The urgency with which I wanted to put on the show in New Delhi was no less than in Lahore, and for precisely the same reasons.

By the time my Peace Campaign exhibition opened in early November 1947, the rioting had stopped, but not the hatred among the communities. The communal conflict had now taken a new turn, resulting in confrontation between the dominions, as the two newly established countries were called during the interim period. The burning question at the time

Plate 49: MOTHER WITH CHILD, TAMIL NADU

Plate 50: MOTHER WITH CHILD, KERALA

was the transfer to Pakistan of the assets that were to be proportionately shared between the two successor states of British India. Nehru's views were in tune with those of Mahatma Gandhi that India was honour-bound to pay what was due to Pakistan. But the Hindu communalists were opposed to it, and they had unleashed a vicious campaign of vilification, calling Mohandas Gandhi "Mohammad Gandhi" and accusing him of being a "fifth columnist" of Pakistan. Sardar Patel, another prominent Congress leader, impugned in a speech the loyalty of all Muslims who had opted to remain in India, and Pandit Nehru was said to be so infuriated that he wanted to dismiss him from his cabinet. Rumours also had it that some right-wing Hindu leaders, supported by fascist-type religious organizations and thousands of corrupt and unprincipled civil and military officers, were only waiting in the wings for a chance to overthrow Pandit Nehru by staging a political *coup d'état*. According to them, Nehru was an "idealist living in the clouds", and his visionary ideas were out of tune with the hard realities. In this climate, the *raison d'être* of my effort had acquired a political connotation in addition to the message of peace and communal harmony which my earlier exhibition in Lahore was designed to convey.

So for political reasons as well, I very much wanted Panditji himself to inaugurate the show, and thus fulfil my long-cherished desire. This wish of mine had become almost an obsession, since I had failed to approach him in Lahore, and here in New Delhi I did not know how to go about it. The several telephone messages I had left with the Prime Minister's secretariat were either not answered or at best the replies were equivocal. Then suddenly another crisis blew up and whatever little hope I harboured about having Panditji open the show was rudely dashed. I was already mounting the pictures when we heard the bad news that thousands of mercenary tribal bands from the North-West Frontier Province had launched a ferocious attack against Kashmir in an attempt to set up a fundamentalist Islamic regime. Following the partition of India, most of the princely states had decided to join either India or Pakistan, but a crisis was created in Kashmir by the failure of its Maharaja to take a decision. The climax was reached when the tribals moved into the valley and almost succeeded in reaching Srinagar and its airport. Maharaja Hari Singh had then appealed for help from India, and Sheikh Abdullah, the popular Kashmiri leader who had been imprisoned by the Maharaja until recently, had arrived in New Delhi for consultations with Pandit Nehru. In the circumstances, my request to Panditji was presumably already in the waste-paper basket,

Plate 51: COAL MINER'S CHILDREN, BIHAR

Plate 52: A *HARIJAN* FAMILY, MAHARASHTRA

Plate 53: *TODA* TRIBESMEN, NILGIRI HILLS

I thought, and it was obviously futile to pursue the matter any further. Hence, the Secretary of the All-India Fine Arts and Crafts Society decided to approach Rajkumari Amrit Kaur, the Health Minister, requesting her to open the exhibition.

The Rajkumari, who had the privilege of becoming the first woman cabinet minister in an independent Government of India, also alluded to communal violence when she opened the exhibition on 3 November 1947. In her inaugural speech, she referred to some of the slogans under which I had grouped my photographs in seven sections, and among other things, stated: "Inhuman sufferings were inflicted on innocent and peaceful people in both parts of the Punjab. But let us now forgive and forget. We should win over others by love and not by weapons. Our country is a beautiful country and let us make it more prosperous by our joint efforts. Our mutual love will again unite us." The method of presentation was similar to that of my previous exhibition in Lahore, as a staff reporter of *The Times of India* also commented. Appreciating the "careful planning" of the exhibition which he thought was "contrary to so many we have had", he reiterated that its main purpose was "to present pictorially life in the Punjab as it used to be before it became the scene of communal strife, and as it is today." I was especially elated by his comment that "no more effective indictment of violence could have been presented." I did not recall having mentioned to anyone the difficulties I had to overcome in mounting the exhibition, and hence I was rather intrigued how the reporter found out that "Judging from the technique of his work, it is difficult to imagine that these photographs were made with economy of material and lack of proper equipment, some even with a borrowed camera." On the whole, I was delighted with the public response and derived great satisfaction from the number of people who came to see the exhibition during the week, surpassing my wildest expectations.

But the greatest surprise of my life was yet to come. It happened a few days before the exhibition was to close when, all of a sudden, Pandit Nehru himself dropped in. There was a great commotion as everyone in the hall rushed towards the entrance in astonishment, whispering, "Panditji has come! Panditji has come!" I was flabbergasted. Nonplussed, I did not know what to do as I was standing at the far end of the hall. This was the great event I had been so eagerly looking forward to for so long and now when it happened, I found myself quite unprepared for the occasion. Having been out all day in the refugee camp, I was not even properly dressed: I was wearing a worn-out sweater over a soiled shirt with an open collar, and in my unpressed trousers, I was hardly presentable. I felt ashamed to meet the Prime Minister of India in my shabby clothes, and my first reaction was to hide behind the crowd that surrounded him from all sides. Meanwhile the Secretary of the Society had spotted me, and tightly grasping me by the arm, he hustled me hurriedly through the gathering and introduced me to Panditji. Joining my hands nervously in a *namaskar,* I stood at a respectable distance and felt very awkward when Pandit Nehru extended his hand to shake. I was so used to seeing the great leader from a distance that it seemed strange that I should touch him. Breathing heavily, I hesitated for a moment as my folded hands seemed glued to each other, before I mustered enough courage to step forward and diffidently shake his hand.

Without saying a word, the Prime Minister then moved in the direction of the exhibits and started walking from one end of the gallery to the other, as I trailed behind him. At first he seemed rather absent-minded, but as he proceeded, his interest in the pictures appeared to grow and he began asking questions about them. One of the seven sections into which I had grouped the photographs was capped by an inscription: *Our country is beautiful; let not the fascists destroy it.* He looked at the caption intently and turning towards me, he lifted his finger, as if he was on the point of saying something; but then he hesitated, and for some reason did not make any comment. By then he was looking more carefully at each picture, and standing in front of *Sunset at a Village* (Plate 30), he seemed especially attracted by its light effect. Noticing his interest, the Secretary of the Society stepped forward and told him that the photograph looked even more beautiful in dim light, and ordered his assistant to turn off the bright overhead lamps in the hall. Indeed, in subdued lighting, the picture acquired a strange luminosity of its own, as the long and slender shadows of village carts and the three peasants walking against the slanting rays of the setting sun produced a marvellous three-dimensional effect. Panditji liked the picture all the more as a symbol of communal harmony as I told him that the photograph showed three friends — a Muslim, a Hindu and a Sikh — coming home together after a hard day's work in the fields. Meanwhile a special assistant of the Prime Minister had rushed in with an urgent note, presumably about Kashmir. Pandit Nehru read it, studied the message for a moment, and then moved on hurriedly to see the remaining few photographs before he walked out of the hall as suddenly as he had come in.

I was at an age of my life when the see-saw of emotions is so precariously balanced between two extremes of love and hate, exaltation and grief, joy and sadness, compassion and

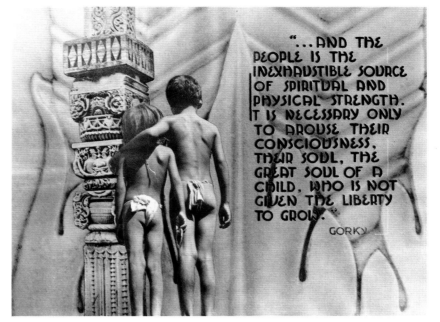

THE ORIGINAL TITLE-PAGE DESIGN OF *THIS MY PEOPLE*   THE COLLAGE WITH A QUOTATION FROM MAXIM GORKY

cruelty, generosity and selfishness, that its planks are easily tilted one way or the other with the slightest provocation. It was the first time that I was personally introduced to Panditji, and the euphoria I felt is difficult to describe. My heart was seething with intense happiness as I went out of the exhibition hall. It was a lovely afternoon, and walking down the street, I skipped from time to time, humming a tune, and smiling broadly at everyone I met. Bubbling with enthusiasm, my heart was singing with joy and my buoyant spirits were sprouting like flowers in the spring-like winter of Delhi. I floated as if in a kind of visionary state in which the deep blue sky, the sound of voices borne by the fresh wind, the birds singing in the trees, and the soft sunlight illuminating the spacious lawns of bungalows through which I passed, all seemed steeped in happiness. It was a wonderful sensation, and only those who have experienced an ecstasy such as this could understand its power. I had finally met my idol, guide and philosopher, the sensitive idealist with modern outlook whose democratic ideas about economic justice, social equality and political freedom, and the policy of non-alignment in international affairs, had captured the imagination of the whole generation to which I belonged.

My mood of exaltation continued to prevail as Sheikh Abdullah also came to visit the

95

exhibition, soon after the Maharaja of Kashmir signed the Instrument of Accession to India. History was in the making and events were racing as fast as the Indian troops that rushed to Kashmir and landed at Srinagar airport. For the Sheikh to find time for my exhibition at this crucial juncture was no less an honour for me than Pandit Nehru's earlier visit. As he had come along with Indira Gandhi, I speculated that perhaps Panditji himself might have mentioned the show to them. Pandit Nehru held Sheikh Abdullah in great esteem and affection, and it was also because of his intervention that at the time the Sheikh headed the newly established Emergency Administration in Kashmir. Impressed with the exhibits, and having learned that my forebears also hailed from Uri in Kashmir, he then personally asked me if I would join the group of progressive writers, artists and journalists whom he had invited to help build up what he called the Kashmir Cultural Front. I was delighted, and without any hesitation accepted the invitation on the spot, notwithstanding that my exams were at hand: in the aftermath of the partition, the venue of the final Master of Science degree examinations for refugee students had been moved from Lahore to New Delhi.

By the time I reached Srinagar the invaders had been repulsed with the help of the Indian Army and were already retreating; but not before they had caused tremendous havoc, murdering, pillaging, looting and burning as they went on the rampage along their trail. My ancestral town of Uri could not be saved from destruction either; the invaders had so thoroughly ransacked the hamlet that as I wandered through the heaps of rubble, I could not find a single building standing. There I also learned about the incredible bravery of Brigadier Ranjit Singh Jamwal, who had sacrificed his life on the Uri front, fighting against the murderous invaders. If it were not for the three crucial days during which his men held up the tribals from reaching Srinagar airport, the Indian Army would have found it difficult to defend the valley. I was particularly excited by the heart-warming display of communal unity, as large numbers of Muslims, Hindus and Sikhs flocked to join the People's Miltia. They had jointly erected a ring of barricades in defence of Srinagar and it was a marvellous sight to see men and women and even children parading the streets as in *Children Playing People's Militia* (Plate 34). Groups of young artists had spontaneously mushroomed, staging plays about communal harmony as seen in *A Student Actress* (Plate 35). Writers and poets were inspired to write on the subject and in particular I was greatly impressed by *A People's Poet* (Plate 33), a Muslim who had written several beautiful lyrics in support of communal amity. "In the engulfing darkness of communal conflict, the only ray of light came from Kashmir," stated Mahatma Gandhi at the time, and it was the kind of future in a secular, united and egalitarian India with which I was greatly inspired.

In the wake of recently won freedom, everything seemed as wonderful as the captivating natural beauty of Kashmir. Even in the bleak light of winter, the landscape was as seductive as an antique Kashmiri carpet. "There are some places where it charms even those who are unprepared for it and comes like the deep notes of a distant and a powerful organ," wrote Pandit Nehru in *The Discovery of India*. "Among these favoured spots is Kashmir where loveliness dwells and an enchantment steals over the senses. It cannot be only because of its magnificent woods, the pure limpidity of its lakes, the splendour of its snowy mountain tops, or the happy murmur of its myriad brooks sounding in the cool soft air. Nor can it be only the grace or majesty of its ancient buildings, though the ruins of Martand rise at the prow of their Karewa as proudly as a Greek temple on a promontory, and the little shrine of Payar, carved out of ten stones, has the perfect proportions of the choragic monuments of Lysicrates. One cannot even say that it comes of the combination of art and landscape, for the fine buildings in a romantic setting are to be found in many other countries. But what is found in Kashmir alone is the grouping of these two kinds of beauty in the midst of a nature still animated with a mysterious life, which knows how to whisper close to our ears and make the pagan depths of us quiver."

The nostalgia for open spaces that I used to feel in captivity, and my fascination with nature and wildlife, had made the place even more enchanting. Often I would rise early in the morning and go out alone for long walks through the streets of Srinagar and along the banks of the river Jhelum. I took several photographs of early-morning scenes as *The Dhabba* (Plate 32), a typical eating place for the ordinary people, where I would often drink cups of delicious Kashmiri tea. As I strolled at random, watching the cold, slow-moving water of the river and the winter mist that hovered above it, I was greatly excited by the phantasmal effect it created. Against the backdrop of the swaying tops of the *chinar* trees, houseboats and *shikaras* seemed to float above the winter mist, and the silhouettes of the hazy mountains, whose snow-covered peaks reflected the soft, amber light of the hidden sun, all created an hypnotic effect on me. Of the many photographs I took, the ones I liked most were those of children. Sometimes they were unaware that I was taking their photographs, as for example, *Child at the Water-tap* (Plate

40). But even otherwise, unlike the adults, they were not camera shy and most of them willingly posed when asked, even naked as in *Children Bathing in the River Jhelum* (Plate 39). I enjoyed watching little boys and girls rowing their small boats as they went out on errands for their elders, like *Girl in a Shikara* (Plate 38).

Of the children's pictures, *The Child of Nature* (Plate 41), was by far my favourite. I had come across this beautiful little girl one morning as I was walking along the bank of the river, when she had suddenly appeared like an angel out of the misty veil that covered the hazy mountains. She stopped walking as she saw me and as she stood there chewing a straw, she made quite a picture in the soft velvet light. Wearing a Kashmiri garb and significantly holding on to a few stems of straw in one hand, her enigmatic look into the uncertainty of the distant future, seemed to articulate the hopes and fears of all the children in our wide-open world. She seemed to be standing on the razor's edge of the present where the misery of the past seemed sharply etched into hope for the future. In my optimistic mood, even the slavery of carpet-weaving and other handicrafts to which many children in Kashmir were yoked, seemed to be a passing phase of the feudal system established by the Maharajas in the past, and which the newly won independence was soon expected to eradicate. Feudalism was so repellent to me that I even ignored my father's advice to go and see in one of the palaces of the Maharaja, some portraits of the royal family that my uncle had painted: my father used to tell me that his elder brother, Kulwant Singh, was a court painter and he believed that in my artistic talents I had taken after my uncle. Instead, I would go into the countryside, taking pictures of Kashmiri peasants. I enjoyed seeing them bask in the sun as in *A Peasant Family* (Plate 45), and also took several posed photographs as *Portrait of a Peasant* (Plate 46) and *Peasant with Grandson* (Plate 47).

I would have loved to stay on longer in Kashmir, had it not been for my impending exams. And I recall how worried I was when I found that the Banihal pass, over which aircraft used to fly to New Delhi, was closed because of a snowstorm. In those days the good old Dakotas could not fly high enough to cross the mountains, so it was only in fine weather that the planes cruised low through the valleys, precariously flanked by high mountain peaks. For ten days in a row I had gone every day to Srinagar airport, hoping for the weather to clear, and finally when it did, there were already so many VIPs waiting that I had no chance of getting a seat. Margaret Bourke-White, the famous photographer, was also among the waiting pas-

Plate 57: A PEASANT WITH BULLOCKS, UTTAR PRADESH

Plate 58: PEASANTS WORKING IN RICE FIELDS, KASHMIR

Plate 59:
A PEASANT SOWING RICE, KASHMIR

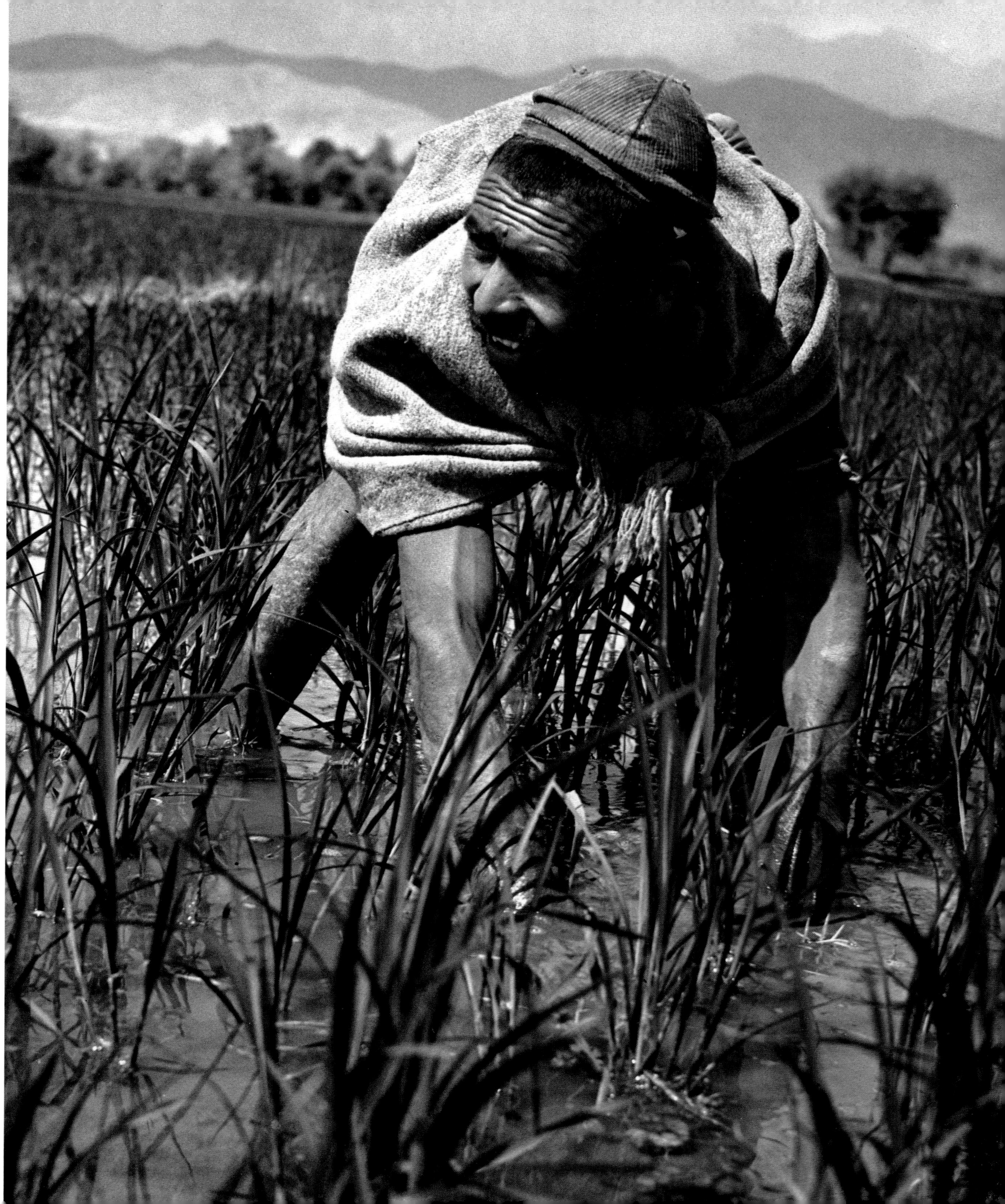

Plate 61: MINE WORKERS, BIHAR

sengers, and I have remained ever indebted to her for having offered her own seat to me even though she had fixed up some important interviews with several Indian leaders. "Your exams are more important than my interview with Jawaharlal Nehru," she said to me, words that have since remained embedded in my memory.

My original plan was to exhibit my pictures of Indian sculptures, soon after my exams were out of the way. But then the unexpected events in Kashmir had intervened so that once again the *Stones that Sing* exhibition had to be postponed. Instead, I decided first to display my Kashmir collection, especially as Sheikh Abdullah had already promised to open the show in response to my request to him in Srinagar. Accordingly, the Kashmir leader kept the appointment in the third week of August 1948, as a staff reporter of *The Hindustan Times* recorded: "Opening an exhibition of photographs by Mr. Madanjeet at Exhibition Hall, New Delhi, on Wednesday, Sheikh Abdullah, Premier of Jammu and Kashmir, said that the artist was one who, out of love of the Kashmiris, had come to help build up the Kashmir Cultural Front last year." He added that "About 100 photographs, neatly arranged and excellently presented, gave an accurate impression of Kashmir's struggle against the tribal invaders from Pakistan. Mr. Madanjeet has taken great pains to combine the artistic and the topical. Each photograph is, in fact, a story by itself." His compliments about my artistic abilities pleased me and in particular I was glad that he also reiterated what other art critics had earlier pointed out that "Mr. Madanjeet is a great exponent of the light and shadow technique. His effects are obtained essentially by contrast."

From the set of pictures that I carried to show Pandit Nehru on that day, I had intentionally excluded all those photographs which explicitly depicted death, arson and destruction. The gruesome scenes I had photographed in Lahore and Amritsar, and recently at Uri in Kashmir, had started evoking schizophrenic memories that I could not stand any longer. Now it was the human factor that I wanted my pictures to project. Poverty was of course inherent in the strata of society which most of my photographs represented, but their *leitmotiv* was not to show poverty for its own sake, but to create a sense of urgency in order to remedy the state of affairs that produced it. Through my photographs, I wanted to make people aware of their collective responsibility, now that India had achieved its freedom. Until then, all the blame was conveniently thrown on the British colonial administration, but now no such handy excuse existed. The authorities of free India were now duty-bound to undertake concrete ac-

104

tion to help the poor, the downtrodden masses who were yearning to breathe freely. How immoral and scandalous it was, I wanted to say, that the people of free India must go on living in the impossible conditions of stark misery and degradation of poverty as seen in several of my photographs such as *Mother with Child* (Plate 49). This photograph I had taken in the outskirts of Madras, and the look of despondency on the face of the mother, trying to shelter her child with both her hands, was as touching as the grown-up appearance of the barely three-year-old Kerala infant in *Mother with Child* (Plate 50).

In brief, I wanted the Congress Government of Independent India to fulfil the pledges its election manifesto had undertaken during the 1946 General Elections. It was a remarkable document which Pandit Nehru had drafted, and an inspiring paragraph of which I still remembered: "The most vital and urgent of India's problems is how to remove the curse of poverty and raise the standards of the masses. It is to the wellbeing and progress of these masses that the Congress has directed its special attention and its constructive activities. It is by their wellbeing and advancement that it has judged every proposal and every change and it has declared that everything that comes in the way of the good of the masses of our country must be removed. Industry and agriculture, the social services and public utilities must be encouraged, modernised and rapidly extended in order to add to the wealth of the country and give it the capacity for self-growth, without dependence on others. But all this must be done with the primary object and paramount duty of benefiting the masses of our people and raising their economic, cultural and spiritual level, removing unemployment, and adding to the dignity of the individual. For this purpose it will be necessary to plan and co-ordinate social advance in all its many fields, to prevent the concentration of wealth and power in the hands of a few individuals and groups, to prevent vested interests inimical to society from growing and to have social control of the mineral resources, means of transport and principal methods of production and distribution in land, industry and in other departments of national activity, so that free India may develop into a co-operative commonwealth."

My mind was crowded with such thoughts as I pedalled my way from Mehrauli to Teen Murti House. By recapitulating past events and all my achievements, I seemed to be trying to generate sufficient self-confidence, and thus convince myself that notwithstanding I was a student, I did merit Pandit Nehru's attention. It was as if I wanted to put my credentials in order before calling on the Prime Minister of India. But the nearer I came to my des-

Plate 65:
PORTRAIT OF
A RAJPUT GIRL,
RAJASTHAN

tination, the less reassured I felt, especially when I found myself among hundreds of clerical members of the secretariat staff who were cycling in the same direction on their way to government offices. In midst of that ant-like swarm of people, I felt like a non-entity as my individuality seemed to have been swallowed up in the multitude. It did not help either as I started cycling at the far edge of the road, in an attempt to demarcate and prevent my identity from being overwhelmed by the crowd, a very petty-bourgeois attitude that sometimes involuntarily took hold of me. I was overawed by the massive red-stone buildings of the government secretariat as I passed through its North and South blocks, and by the time I reached Teen Murti House, which had been until recently the residence of the British Commander-in-Chief in India, my self-confidence had evaporated.

In those days Pandit Nehru lived in an open house where anybody could walk in. People used to say that there were two historic landmarks in India which the tourist came to see — one was the Taj Mahal and the other Pandit Nehru. As I approached the out-house on one side of the large iron-grilled gateway, I saw two security guards sitting behind a small wooden table. They were busy drinking tea in glass tumblers tightly held in both hands, and were obviously enjoying its warmth as they leisurely chatted with each other. They looked at me indif-

Plate 66: LANDSCAPE, TAMIL NADU

ferently from the corner of their eyes, and casually waved me in as they continued sipping the beverage with audible slurps. The only reason for my visit I gave them was that I wanted to see Panditji, as if it were some kind of password with which any Tom, Dick or Harry could enter the Prime Minister's residence. They did not even ask me what was wrapped up in the packet that was tied on the rear carrier of my bicycle. Pushing my bike by the handle-bars, I walked up the slope of the side road that led to the porch, when suddenly I saw behind the trees a large group of people who had gathered in the lawn facing the house. They had come for Panditji's *darshan*, a daily routine in which all kinds of people would come for "spiritual audience" with Pandit Nehru, even if they had nothing to tell him. The Prime Minister used to meet with them briefly, exchanging pleasantries as he came out of the house on his way to the office.

Good Lord! I said to myself. How can I possibly meet with Panditji in this crowd? Even if I succeed in drawing his attention, how shall I be able to show him the pictures, standing in the midst of this multitude? Moreover, I recoiled from the awful thought of being humiliated in public, should he turn down my request. "What will people say?" had haunted me since infancy. As a child, when I did not wash myself or brush my teeth properly, soiled my clothes, neglected to do my homework, failed to obtain good grades at school, or anything else under the sun which I was required to do, the question which my parents asked was invariably, "What will people say?" What the stigma actually implied, I never really understood; all I knew was that it must be something terrible as the fear of people's opinion deterred me from many things that I would otherwise have done. Only in a socially disintegrated society do people not care about what others think, my mother would tell me — a very democratic attitude. The tenacity with which such childhood inhibitions stick is really incredible, even though I try very hard to shake them off, as I attempted in vain to do that morning. My enthusiasm sagged and I was so discouraged and demoralized that I was on the point of giving up by the time I walked up to the porch of the house.

Then as luck would have it, by chance I met a young housekeeper as I was wheeling my bicycle around towards the exit. Her curiosity was aroused by the photographs I was carrying, and having seen some of them, she also felt that the subject was close to Panditji's heart. So she very kindly led me into the waiting room on the ground floor, and suggested that I should mark time there until the Prime Minister came down on his way to office. A number of sofas were lined up along both sides of the walls, and as I sat down on one of them near the entrance, I could see the staircase at the far end of the room which descended from the second-floor living quarters. Unwrapping the old sheets of newspaper with which the album was covered, I placed it on the low wooden table in front of the sofa, prominently displaying the title cover which I had taken considerable pains to design: it was a photograph of a bas-relief in plasticine representing two faces of a peasant couple, a plaque that I had sculpted myself, and beneath was printed the title *This, My People* (Plate 55). The title-page photograph was spliced on a thick cardboard piece and under it I had placed an equally large sheet of plain unexposed photographic paper, on which I expected Panditji to write a few lines if he acceded to my request.

Immediately below the plain sheet of paper, I had inserted a reproduction of a collage in three layers which, I thought, made an appropriate frontispiece as it was designed to convey the spirit of the collection (Plate 56). Against the background of a marble plaque at the Taj Mahal — a bas-relief with motifs of lotus leaves and flowers — was superimposed a cutout of a richly ornamented pillar I had photographed in one of the Qutub Minar pavilions, and in the foreground were two poverty-stricken children of mill workers at Coimbatore. Inscribed on it were also a few lines of a quotation from *Mother*, a novel by Maxim Gorky: "We shall win because we are with the working people. Our power to work, our faith in the victory of truth, we obtain from the people. And the people are an inexhaustible source of spiritual and physical strength. In them are vested all possibility, and with them everything is attainable. It is necessary only to arouse their consciousness, the great soul of a child, who is not given the liberty to grow." Through this simple collage, I wanted to convey the entirety of what I had seen and felt during my recent travels, a kind of summary of all my ideals and emotions, which I thought Panditji must take into account in his foreword to my set of photographs. In my youthful enthusiasm, I somehow wanted to give a hint to Panditji about the slant which he might wish to give in his preface.

Wasn't I taking too much for granted? What if Panditji did not even recognize me? Doubts began creeping into my mind as I waited. Of course he would! Surely he could not have possibly forgotten his visit to my Peace Campaign exhibition. But that was more than a year ago, and Pandit Nehru met so many people every day. All kinds of contradictory thoughts crossed my mind. Should he not first of all see some of the familiar pictures in order

Plate 67: A VEGETABLE GARDEN, NILGIRI HILLS

Plate 68: POTATO HARVEST, NILGIRI HILLS

to refresh his memory? Again I lifted the cover, and felt that it would look rather odd should Panditji see a plain sheet of paper as he opened the album. So I removed the blank sheet and put it beneath all the other photographs, trying at the same time to pick out a suitable picture to place on the very top. In my confusion, I could not make up my mind as I shuffled the photographs over again, and at the same time looking towards the staircase, lest Panditji should come down in the meantime. Finally I decided on *Sunset at a Village*, because it was the picture Pandit Nehru had particularly admired at the exhibition. Moreover the subject had strong emotional overtones because it depicted the peaceful environment of communal harmony, an ideal for which Mahatma Gandhi had sacrificed his life only a few months earlier. So even if Pandit Nehru would not recall the picture *per se*, I thought, its emotional impact would surely revive old memories.

The longer I waited, the more fidgety I became. I felt very nervous, repeatedly rehearsing the phrases I had composed in my mind to say to Panditji. Over and over again I memorized the sentences, and each time I forgot some essential point I wanted to tell him. My mind seemed almost blank: it was the kind of sensation I usually experienced when sitting for an exam, as though I had forgotten everything despite all the books I had crammed during the previous night. Every second seemed like an hour, and the longer I waited, the faster I felt my heart beat. Then to my great discomfort, I saw another man come into the room. Clad in an all-white *khadi*, and wearing a Gandhi cap, he gave the impression of being a very important politician; it meant that my chances of meeting with Panditji had become more remote. Surely, I feared, he would elbow me out during the short time the Prime Minister had at his disposal. So in order to draw Pandit Nehru's attention before he met the VIP, I moved towards another set of sofas nearer the staircase in order to stay at the head of the queue. Then my heart sank, as two more persons entered, also attired in hand woven-cloth called *khadi*, a symbol of nationalistic patriotism since Mahatma Gandhi championed the revival of village industries, but which was already turning into a uniform for self-seeking sycophants. Now I moved to yet another couch that was almost facing the staircase, and placing the album on the table in front, kept standing so that Panditji would not ignore my presence.

At last, I saw the Prime Minister coming down the staircase. My heart missed a beat and in my confusion, instead of stepping forward to greet him, I turned back quickly towards the table in order to pick up the album. He stopped abruptly, and waited momentarily as he stood half way up the staircase, until he could see my face: his spontaneous reaction of caution was natural as it was less than a year, on 30 January, that Mahatma Gandhi had been shot dead by a Hindu fanatic at his evening prayer meeting in New Delhi. He looked at me intently as I lifted the album, and then having recognized me or perhaps my familiar face, he stepped down smiling.

"*Ye kya hai ?* " (What is it?) he asked in Hindi.

"Panditji," I said, and mumbled something incoherently, holding out the album so that he could see the title.

"This My People." Pandit Nehru read it aloud, characteristically tilting his head on one side. "Let me see," he said, and taking the album in both his hands, he walked towards the nearest sofa and sat down, placing the pictures on the table in front. As he lifted the cover and saw *Sunset at a Village*, he indicated with a motion of his hand that I may sit down beside him. Out of respect for the Prime Minister, I remained standing. But when he asked me the second time, I sat down on the edge of the sofa at a respectable distance. I watched his face, trying to figure out if he recollected the picture, as he kept looking at it for quite some time. So I was encouraged to ask him whether he remembered having seen it at my exhibition.

"Yes I do," he said, and added to my intense delight that he even recalled "the fine effect it created in the dim light". That put me at ease, and helped to relieve the tension that had built up in me to breaking point.

Pandit Nehru then began looking at the pictures, slowly turning one leaf after the other and asking several questions about the people and the places where they had been photographed. He looked with great interest at several pictures of Kashmiri peasants working in rice fields, and in particular *A Peasant with Bullocks* (Plate 57), and *Peasants Rotating a Water-wheel* (Plate 54), photographs which I had taken in Uttar Pradesh. I scanned his face intently, and noticed some remarkable changes of expression as he turned from one sheet to another. The grim contortions of his face clearly reflected the plight of the people sleeping in a Calcutta street, and the wretchedness of the poor woman sheltering her child, whom I had photographed in Madras. His face was tense when he saw *Labourer Pushing a Cart* (Plate 60) in Kashmir; and *Portrait of a Mill Worker* (Plate 10) in Coimbatore. He seemed especially touched by several pictures of refugees, as their ordeal was still a burning issue. But then the wrinkles on his brow disappeared and an expression of serene tranquillity descended on his

countenance as he looked at pictures of beautiful women such as *Portrait of a Rajput Girl* (Plate 65). He was glad to see the two Rajasthani women swinging in *Swing of Sawan* (Plate 64). The picture reminded him, he said, of the songs written by Amir Khusrau that are still widely sung in towns and villages of northern India, especially during the rainy season when swings are hung from the branches of *mango* and *peepal* trees and all the girls and boys gather together to celebrate the season. He was bemused to see the photograph in which four women walked behind their menfolk in the *Landscape* in Maharashtra (Plates 5a and 5b), and remarked: "Isn't it typical of our machismo towards women?" He enquired about the location of the pictures I had taken on my father's estate in the Nilgiris as seen in *A Vegetable Garden* (Plate 67) and *Potato Harvest* (Plate 68). And he was delighted with the carefree beaming smiles on the faces of *Children in a Wheat Farm* (Plate 2); *Fishermen's Children* (Plate 69); and *The Future of Mankind* (Plate 92).

It was time for the Prime Minister to go to his office. His aide was already waiting at the door, trying to draw his attention by frequently looking at his watch. The three visitors had been fretting impatiently for quite some time, as they paced up and down the corridor that led to the entrance. There was of course also the crowd of people waiting outside for his *darshan*. But Pandit Nehru took his own time, so absorbed had he become in the pictures. He seemed so far away, even though I sat so close to him. By then, he was looking at the collage with Gorky's inscription, and as he seemed impressed by the quotation, I got the impression that I had succeeded in making my point. So I took this opportunity of handing him the plain sheet of paper and requested him if he would be kind enough to write a few lines by way of a preface to my collection? "Yes, I shall try," he responded briefly and handing over the album to his secretary, he rose from the couch. And as he was walking out of the room, the waiting politicians rushed towards him and stooped low to touch his feet. Pandit Nehru recoiled, took a step backward and rebuked them, saying: "Never ever do that again!" He then made his way towards the crowd gathered outside.

A day passed, then two and three and four, and I did not hear anything more from the Prime Minister's residence. As there was no telephone at Gurbaksh Singh's house in Mehrauli, I had left the telephone number of Photo Service Company with Pandit Nehru's secretary. There I kept vigil, enquiring several times a day if any communication had been received from Teen Murti House and often waited personally, marking time near the telephone. With my

PANDIT NEHRU AT EXHIBITION

✳✳✳

Photographs and Sketches of Indian Antiquities

(By Our Art Critic)

Pandit Jawaharlal Nehru, the Afghan Ambassador and numerous other well known personalities of Delhi society were present at an exhibition of photographs and drawings by Madanjeet, organized yesterday afternoon at the Exhibition Hall in Parliament Street, by the All-India Fine Arts and Crafts Society.

Madanjeet, some of whose admirable photographs have appeared in *The Statesman*, has just returned from a long tour of India, during which he visited some of the most famous antiquities and shrines of this country. His 'bag' is a superb collection of photographs, mainly of ancient Indian sculpture, from Mamallapuram to Gandhara, and from Ellora to Khajuraho. The quality of these photographs is really admirable: the stone and bronze of these ancient sculptures speak to the spectator with an almost uncanny force, and many of the detail-pictures show us angles which an ordinary visitor to these often dark temples might never have been able to see.

Madanjeet is both a fine artist and an aesthetically sensitive person; witness not only his prints, but also a number of his fine drawings after ancient sculptures, in which he succeeds in capturing the essential vision of the artist in a few telling lines.

The Statesman: New Delhi, 16 February 1949.

Plate 70: LANDSCAPE, SIWALIK HIMALAYA

youthful impatience the telephone made me jump each time it rang, expecting it to be the message. Especially at that age, indeterminate waiting of this kind really got on my nerves, an unbearable feeling verging on some kind of a mental psychotic disorder that I seemed to have developed while in prison, where time stretched from minutes into hours, and from hours into days and nights, and then started all over again. It was not until the morning of the fifth day that the long-awaited call came through at last, informing me that Panditji would receive me that day at seven in the evening. I was delighted. Greatly elated, I cycled all the way back to Mehrauli, proudly telling all my friends about the good news. Having changed into "decent" clothes, I pedalled back to New Delhi, hours before the appointment. Somehow on that day, the distance between Mehrauli and Teen Murti House did not seem so long and tedious.

I reached Teen Murti House on the dot, and was immediately ushered into the reception room, where three or four visitors were already waiting. I joined them, taking my seat on the very sofa where I had the honour of sitting with Panditji five days earlier. Contrary to the anxious edginess I had felt the other day, today I was relaxed, and did not care how long it took for the other visitors to meet with the Prime Minister before I was able to see him. In fact I was hoping that I would be the last person to see Panditji, thus allowing me more time to spend with him. Looking out towards the spacious lawn at the rear of the house, my heart was gladdened to see the numerous flowerbeds with which it was laid. Winter in Delhi is like spring, and I found it so strange that I had failed to notice the abundance of colourful flowers a few days earlier, nor with all my love for animals had my eyes seen the pandas, the two beautiful creatures which the Chinese had presented to Pandit Nehru. They were chewing something as they sat together clinging to a branch of the tree outside. The mind seems to have its own curtain to shut out the view at will, even if the window to the vision is kept open. It was like taking a photograph with a camera with no film. I was thus reminded to check once again if the camera that I had specially carried on that day was loaded as I very much wanted to take a photograph of Panditji, should the opportunity arise.

As I was hoping, I was the last visitor to be conducted to the room upstairs, in which Pandit Nehru used to work at home after office hours. His aide opened the door very quietly, and I saw him sitting behind a large desk facing the entrance, and engrossed in reading something. In the silence of the room, he did not notice me as I came in; and I stood there quite some time, not wishing to disturb him. Resting his head on his right hand, he made quite a picture in his maroon *sherwani* with a red rose tucked in its button-hole. His torso was sharply defined against the dark backdrop of wooden panels that lined the walls, his face illuminated by a tall flexible table lamp with a black narrow shade. A bouquet of flowers in a glass vase that stood in front of him on the table enhanced his complexion as it reflected a soft hue on his countenance. It was too good a chance to miss, and I could not resist the temptation of focusing the camera on him and snapping a photograph (frontispiece). The light of the flash bulb made him sit up, and raising his head he said, "Hello, Madanjeet!" That was the first time he addressed me by name, and I was overcome with emotion to hear the two words. Then he asked me whether I wanted to take another photograph, wearing his cap, for he rarely appeared in public without the so-called Gandhi cap. And while I was busy taking some more shots from different angles, there was another surprise in store for me as he suddenly enquired about my educational qualifications and the kind of career I wanted to pursue? The question was so unexpected that I was at a loss to reply. I hesitated for a moment and then told him frankly that before deciding on any profession, first of all I wanted to go abroad for higher studies. He did not pursue the subject. Instead, he reached for my album, which was lying at the edge of the table, picked it up, and handing it over to me, said in a soft voice, "I have written the preface; I hope you like it."

Naturally, I was anxious to see what Panditji had written, but I refrained from doing so in his presence, knowing how busy he was. So as soon as I came out of the room and removed the title cover, I was astonished by what I saw. Instead of a few lines that I thought he would have dictated to his stenographer and have typed on the sheet of paper I gave him, he had neatly filled up the entire sheet in his own handwriting. Beautifully written with a fine pen in light blue-ink, he had carefully centred the text in the middle of the page without any correction whatsoever. I was thrilled. Almost running down the staircase, I sat down on the couch where I had waited earlier, and in my eagerness to take in everything all at once, I glanced through the whole page, reading sentences at random — at the end of which was his signature: *Jawaharlal Nehru*, and the date: *New Delhi — January 9, 1949*. The throbbing in my heart having subsided, I then read the full text word by word.

India is frequently represented by pictures of its noble buildings and its famous monuments of antiquity. Sometimes we see more modern structures, which may be impres-

sive in their own ways, but are seldom noted for their grace and beauty.

We have also pictures of her mountains and lakes and forests, and vast plains, and great rivers and ranging torrents and bubbling brooks. All that is India, or a part of India. It is impossible to compress the infinite variety of India in a book or in a collection of pictures. Latterly, the politicians of India appear almost daily in some pose or the other in the newspapers. They compete, in this respect, with the film stars of other countries. It is not a happy development. But that too is India.

Then we have pictures of parties and receptions, especially in New Delhi, with the same people, or more or less the same people, going from one reception to another. They represent the official world as well as the non-official of note and substance, with their wives and daughters. That too is India.

But here in this volume there is a different aspect of India — the common folk, the masses, the people. Again, they represent odd types, chosen from Kashmir in the north to Kanyakumari in the far south. It might have been possible to choose an entirely different set of types and they would have been equally representative of this wonderful country of ours. But this set of pictures does give an idea of our people in the humbler ranks of society. The pictures are good and I hope that many would derive pleasure from them and some understanding, as I have done.

As I sat reading the text, I happened to meet Indira Gandhi as she came in the house from outside. She went out of her way to tell me how late in the night her father had worked writing the preface. Later, I was also informed by Panditji's stenographer that the text was written at about midnight, after the Prime Minister had finished dictating to him the monthly letter that he circulated among the Chief Ministers of all the states in India, informing them of the latest national and international developments.

How extraordinary, I thought, that such an extremely busy person should find so much time and take such pains to oblige a mere student whom he hardly knew, while so many other boisterous busybodies would not even look at such things. It seemed as if the less a person had to do, the more he pretended to be occupied. I was extremely touched by the indulgence which the Prime Minister had shown towards a nobody like me, a convincing measure of Panditji's towering greatness. And yet, I was not entirely happy with the text. I had a mixed

124

feeling about the slant he gave it because it was not in tune with the kind of ideas I had in mind. It appeared as though he had completely ignored Gorky's quotation inscribed on my collage, to which I had purposely drawn his attention. In particular I did not like the expression "odd types", for my intention was not to portray human oddities living on the fringe of our so-called high society, but to emphasize the central role which these unfortunate masses must play in nation-building. Thanks to these people, I would have liked him to say, India had succeeded in achieving her Independence, and now without their wholehearted support, it was inconceivable for our country to march forward towards material and spiritual greatness. They were the reservoir of our inherent, potential strength that must be consolidated, rather than dissipated by letting their lives simply waste away in the isolation and misery of the country's remote villages. I could not comprehend Panditji's equivocal emphasis on different strata of society in a manner that seemed to equivocate the masses with the kind of people "going from one reception to another".

Of course, I realized that Pandit Nehru could not have possibly condensed

Plate 72: WORKERS REPAIRING A WOODEN BRIDGE, LADAKH

Plate 73: A VILLAGE CHIEF OF THIKSE, LADAKH

Plate 74: CHILDREN OF LEH, LADAKH

Plate 76: WOMEN SPECTATORS, LADAKH

in a brief foreword all that he might have wished to say. In his books, there were passage after passage describing his contact with the people, their problems, their vicissitudes, their strivings, their dreams and ambitions. Or was it, I wondered, that it was now my turn to be in that radical grip of revolutionary ethos and fermenting idealism of the younger age, at which Panditji had written in *An Autobiography* : "Looking at them and their misery and overwhelming gratitude, I was filled with shame and sorrow, shame at our easygoing and comfortable life and our petty politics of the city which ignored this vast multitude of semi-naked sons and daughters of India, sorrow at their degradation and overwhelming poverty. A new picture of India seemed to rise before me, naked, starving, crushed and utterly miserable. And their faith in us, casual visitors from the distant city, embarrassed me and filled me with a new responsibility that frightened me." These were the kind of things that I would have liked Panditji to have written, ideas which were the *raison d'être* of my abiding affection for him. Hence my feelings at the time were a strange mixture of excitement diluted

Plate 77: SUNRISE AT LEH, LADAKH

with disappointment; they were like a deep pool — warm and agitated on the surface, but cool and calm at the bottom.

Could it be, I speculated, that it was the beginning of the so-called politics of consensus that is attributed to Pandit Nehru soon after he became Prime Minister of independent India? His slogan "unity in diversity" was the one from which the people of India had essentially derived the strength to combat foreign domination, and now that India had achieved its freedom, unity in diversity seemed to have acquired a different connotation. From the sabre of confrontation, now the emphasis was on unity as the fulcrum of peaceful coexistence on which Pandit Nehru wished to establish India's national stability as well his policy of non-alignment in international affairs. Perhaps Mahatma Gandhi's assassination was the watershed that had convinced him that in India, the battle against communalism, regionalism and casteism, could not be fought with the politics of confrontation. In an essentially conservative society, his socio-economic programmes could only be implemented through a policy of co-operation and not confrontation as the Marxist theory of class struggle implied. Or was it, I wondered, that it was just another case of old wine in new bottles, for this kind of pragmatism in Pandit Nehru's views was not entirely new. As early as 1935, while he was imprisoned in the district jail of Almora, he had pointed out: "It is obvious that the vast changes which socialism envisages cannot be brought about by the sudden passing of a few laws . . . a clash of interest seems inevitable. There is no middle path." And in the same chapter: "It is absurd to say that we will not co-operate with or compromise with others. Life and politics are much too complex for us always to think in straight lines. Even the implacable Lenin said that 'to march forward without compromise, without turning from the path, was intellectual childishness and not the serious tactics of a revolutionary class'. If we are clear about our principles and objectives, temporary compromises will not harm. But the danger lies in our slurring over these principles and objectives — to mislead is far worse than to offend."

As it turned out, it was not until I went on a scholarship to Rome that I realized how right Panditji was in having written the preface in the manner he did. In Italy I discovered to my discomfiture that India's image in the West was a black-and-white cliché of wretched poverty on the one hand and the exotic glamour of the rich Maharajas on the other. If ever there was a digression from this obsession, the news media went no further than to project the glories of the Raj, as if India was still a British colony. It made me mad how little the people

Plate 78: RITUAL DANCE AT HEMIS MONASTERY, LADAKH

in Europe knew or cared about India's freedom movement, her socio-economic problems, and even about her art and culture. I reacted strongly against this callous attitude, the reason why I went on postponing the publication of *This My People*, and instead concentrated on several books on Indian art and culture that were subsequently published in Europe and in the United States. Ashamed of India's poverty, I attempted to cover it up by its rich antiquities. *Nati*, the stone sculpture that I had discovered in Ranganathan temple at Srirangam appeared in my first book, *Indian Sculpture in Bronze and Stone*, published by the Institute of Middle and Far East in Rome. Ironically, this beautiful figure was now trying to cover up the muck of poverty from under which I had pulled her out, in much the same manner of the starving woman with four children whom I had seen trying to hide her misery from public view at Coimbatore railway station — an attitude against which I had then reacted so strongly.

By relating some information given to me by one of Panditji's personal assistants, now it became clear to me that the comprehensive picture of India that he outlined in his preface to *This My People*, was done on purpose, because he knew already that the set of photographs was likely to be published abroad. The person who informed me about how late in the night Panditji had worked in order to write the preface, had also revealed to me in confidence that the day after he wrote it, the Prime Minister had personally telephoned Maulana Abul Kalam Azad, the Education Minister, suggesting that I may be granted a scholarship to go abroad for higher studies. That was also the impression I gathered when I showed Panditji's manuscript to Maulana Azad when he came to Italy in the early fifties, for he knew already who I was and seemed familiar with my work. A great scholar in Persian and Arabic languages, it was a great treat listening to the colourful phrases of his articulate Urdu, as he went visiting Italian monuments and historical sites. Walking through the ruins of Pompeii, he said, "Communal passion is like the burning lava of Vesuvius, the volcano which destroyed this flourishing town. Partitions do not unify; they create more divisions. Those who believe that religious affinity could unite areas that were geographically apart and linguistically different, are swimming against the cultural current of history. Mohammad Ali Jinnah should have known better, for the father of Pakistan himself could not speak Urdu, one of the Indian languages which Pakistan adopted as its own national language." I recalled these prophetic words many years later when Bangladesh separated from Pakistan.

Soon after the visit of Maulana Azad, Pandit Nehru also came to Italy and I felt the

Plate 79: AN UNEMPLOYED GRADUATE, NEW DELHI

warmth of his affection through small gestures and considerations. I interpreted for him in Italian as he landed at Ciampino, the old airport of Rome, and he wanted me to accompany him to all the official functions as his interpreter. When he was about to call on the Italian President, the protocol informed him that my presence was not required because the Palace had its own interpreter. "Does the Palace interpreter know Hindustani?" he enquired and asked me to come along on that plea. But as we sat down with President Gronchi, Panditji began as usual to speak in English, so that my role was reduced to that of a mere spectator. Later, I joined the Foreign Service on his recommendation and once when there was resistance by some envious government officials in India to my proposal to show Indian painters at the *Biennale* International Art Exhibition in Venice, he intervened personally to let me go ahead. For the some forty young Indian painters who exhibited with me, the venture turned out to be a singular success.

    This My People had well established the link of my personal relationship with Pandit Nehru, and I was not surprised that he was among the prominent people who came to see my *Stones that Sing* exhibition of photographs and drawings, which was finally organized a few months before my departure for Italy. He brought along with him Dorothy Norman, the American writer who was his house-guest at the time, and they spent a lot of time admiring the pictures and sketches in the gallery of All-India Fine Arts and Crafts Society, where this exhibition was also arranged. Now, I no longer felt the nervous uncertainty about how the media might react, as I had become used to their favourable reviews. About this exhibition, the art critic of *The Statesman* wrote: "Madanjeet, some of whose admirable photographs have appeared in *The Statesman*, has just returned from a long tour of India, during which he visited some of the most famous antiquities and shrines of this country. His 'bag' is a superb collection of photographs, mainly of ancient Indian sculpture, from Mamallapuram to Gandhara, from Ellora to Khajuraho. The quality of these photographs is really admirable; the stones and bronzes of these ancient sculptures speak to the spectator with an almost uncanny force, and many of the detail-pictures show us angles which the ordinary visitor to these often dark temples might never have been able to see." But already, I seemed to be undergoing a mental metamorphosis, and such tributes no longer created in me the kind of excitement I had felt earlier. I began to miss those uncontrollable emotional impulses that had inspired me to struggle in midst of my agonizing ordeal, the intensity of passion with which I had mounted my Peace Exhibitions in Lahore and New Delhi. Everything in life appeared to be so relative.

138

Plate 81: CHILDREN GOING TO SCHOOL, KASHMIR

Plate 82: CHILDREN AT SCHOOL, PUNJAB

Soon after my *Stones that Sing* exhibition, Pandit Nehru visited Ladakh, the area which the Indian Army had recently cleared of invaders from Pakistan. Obviously impressed by my effort, he asked me to accompany him, so that the pictures that I took during that memorable trip were essentially supplementary to the ones I had taken earlier in the Kashmir valley. I had heard about this vast, stony desert at a very high altitude, but not until I landed in a Dakota on an improvised airstrip along the sandy bank of the Indus passing through Leh at eleven thousand feet, that I realized the awe-inspiring beauty of the region. Here, the great river Indus was only a small rivulet and seemed as disproportionate when compared with the vast history and culture of the Punjab it symbolized, as the rickety wooden bridge (Plate 72), that spanned over all the myth and legend and song and tradition of the age-old culture flowing through this narrow stream of water. Mile after mile of dry rocky boulders formed by melting glaciers, rose grotesquely into gigantic mountain peaks covered with perpetual snows, and contrary to what I imagined, the area was neither uninhabited nor bleak. At dawn and at sunset, I saw some fantastic displays of theatrical lights as recorded in *Sunrise at Leh* (Plate 77). It came as a revelation to me that the ever-changing colour of the dry rocky desert which was basically like that of an elephant hide, was not as monotonous as the moist, lush-green wilderness of perpetual vegetation that always bored me in the tropical climate of the Nilgiris.

In Leh too there was a spectacular display of colours as the people of Ladakh, wearing their traditional costumes, flocked to welcome Pandit Nehru. For the peace-loving Buddhists, the battle of Kashmir was not just a military operation, but a struggle against religious bigotry. They were greatly inspired by the impressive victory which the secular forces of communal co-operation had recently won over aggressive fundamentalist divisiveness. This mood was reflected on the smiling faces of the men, women and children, despite the hardship of their life in the isolation of the region's barren land masses. Hundreds of people had lined up to see Pandit Nehru as we rode on ponies up to the monastery at Hemis, and along the route, I took several photographs of men, women and children. *Children of Leh* (Plate 74) was a group I photographed as they welcomed Pandit Nehru at Leh airstrip; *Sister and Brother* (Plate 71) was an interesting picture I took against the background of Leh monastery; *A Village Chief of Thikse* (Plate 73) was the elder who received the Prime Minister at the monastery of Thikse; and the *Women Spectators* (Plate 76) were those who had lined up at a vantage point in Hemis in order to get a glimpse of the Indian leader. They had all come dressed in their colourful clothes

in order to watch a show of traditional masked dances which had been arranged in the main courtyard of the Hemis monastery as seen in *Ritual Dance at Hemis Monastery* (Plate 78).

It was Pandit Nehru who first gave me the idea about compiling a book on the art of the Himalaya. He was greatly impressed by the scope and grandeur of the paintings he saw in some of the monasteries, and expressed concern at their rapidly deteriorating condition. Looking at the *Jataka* stories painted on the walls in Hemis monastery, he admired in particular the Buddha's Great Renunciation and said that it was incredible how people with hardly any resources could produce such magnificent works of art. Perhaps it was a casual remark, but somehow I felt as though it was a challenge thrown at me. The words began to nag at me, and thus the idea germinated in my mind to compile a book on the subject. In fact, the reproduction of the painting, Great Renunciation, in my book, *Himalayan Art*, was from the same photograph I had taken at that time in Hemis, and I always thought how satisfying a moment it would be to point this out to Panditji when eventually I presented the book to him. But unfortunately Pandit Nehru had died by the time it was published by Unesco. The disappointment I felt was all the more painful, knowing how passionately he loved the Himalayan regions.

During the brief periods Pandit Nehru was released from the nine long years he spent in prison, the first thing he invariably did was to go and spend a few days in the Himalayan regions before resuming his political activities. In *The Discovery of India*, his partiality towards the mountains is thus described: "All of us, I suppose, have varying pictures of our native land and no two persons will think exactly alike. When I think of India, I think of many things: of broad fields dotted with innumerable small villages; of towns and cities I have visited; of the magic of the rainy season which pours life into the dry parched-up land, converting it suddenly into a glistening expanse of beauty and greenery; of people, individually and in mass; and above all, of the Himalayas, snow-capped, or some mountain valley in Kashmir in the spring, covered with new flowers, and with a brook bubbling and gurgling through it. We make and preserve the pictures of our choice, and so I have chosen this mountain background, rather than the more normal picture of a hot, sub-tropical country." Thinking of all this, and especially his genuine appreciation for art and everything that was beautiful, I felt the excruciating pain in my heart for not having completed the book before he died. It turned out to be the greatest regret of my life.

Was that the reason, I sometimes wonder, that after Pandit Nehru's death, something snapped in my soul and I never ever felt like writing another book on art. Somehow I could not shake off a kind of "neuronic inertia", which according to Sigmund Freud, works in the unconscious towards the reduction of any tension that can be identified with an accumulation of "energy". It appeared to be a strange psychological complex in which the bondage of my deep-seated political and personal attachment to Panditji had become emotionally inseparable from my creative activity. Since he wrote the preface to *This My People*, all my work in the sphere of Indian art was not only inspired, but personally encouraged by him. His introduction to my first publication in the Unesco World Art series created a powerful surge of encouragement that was as overwhelming as its devastating reaction when that inspiration departed with him. His death seemed to have extinguished the fire of stimulation in my heart and sapped me of the driving spirit which had given me the strength to slog for years along the dizzy heights of some of the remotest monasteries in the mountains when I was compiling *Himalayan Art*, my second Unesco book. It was as though I wanted to prove myself to be worthy of being his "young colleague", as he referred to me in his introduction to *India, Paintings from Ajanta Caves*, "who has brought his ability and labour to the performance of this task".

Or was it because, by that time, I did not feel the need to camouflage my country's poverty with Indian art and culture? I was still ashamed of India's poverty, but not with the nationalistic egoism of my younger days. Poverty had since become a world phenomenon, in which a billion people constituting every fifth human being on this planet live in humiliating deprivation. The terrible virus of poverty has spread beyond the borders of the so-called Third World, infecting even the most affluent countries. Even in the United States of America, "At any given moment, about one child in four is born poor, and about ten years ago, America became the first nation in history in which the poorest group in the population was the children," stated Daniel P. Moynihan, chairman of the U.S. Senate's subcommittee on social security and family policy. The latest report of the U.S. Census Bureau has revealed that some 32.5 million people live in poverty and about 3 million are homeless. The terrible reality of some 5,000 beggars and stunted children roaming the streets of Chicago and New York City is much more offensive to my sense of social justice than ten times their number in Calcutta, Manila, Cairo or Mexico City. Today *This My People* represents not only the have-nots in India but all the millions of people in an increasingly interdependent world of ours at large.

Plate 85: A FATHER TEACHING HIS SON, PUNJAB

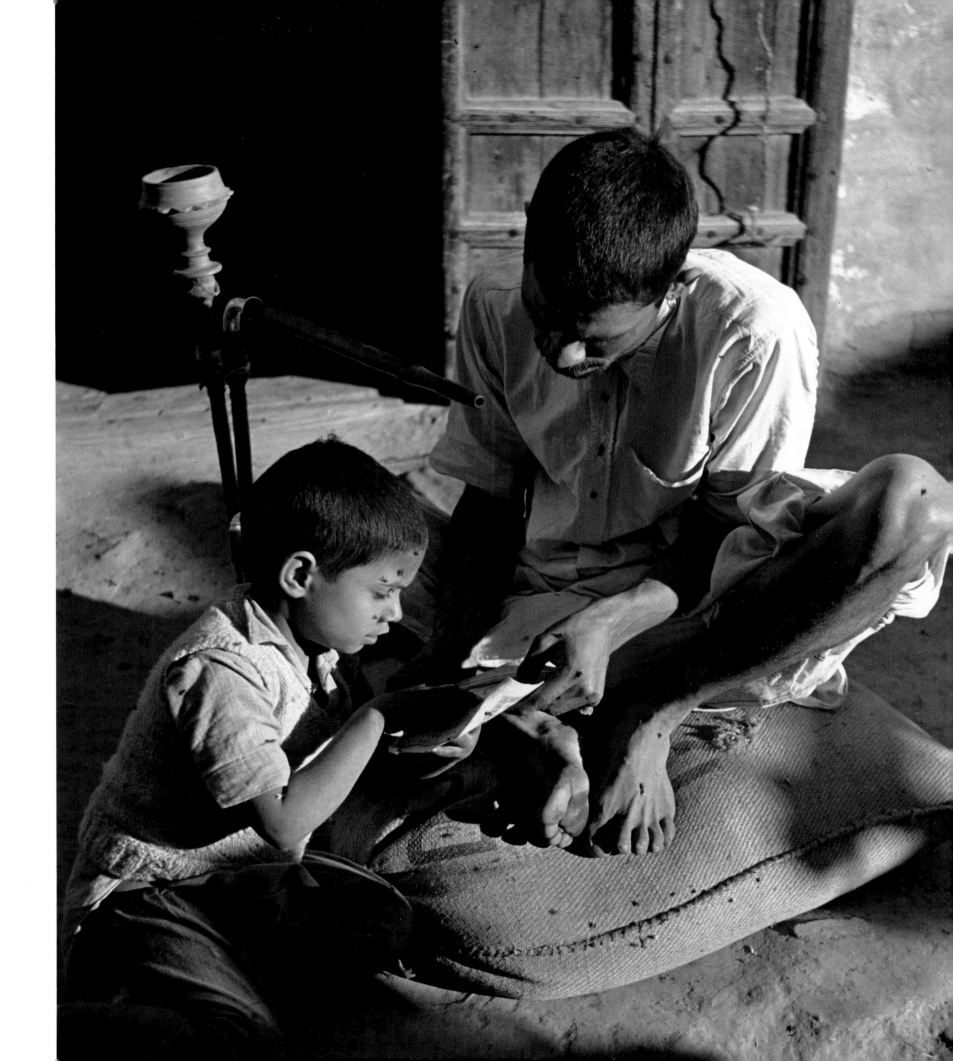

A global crisis of this magnitude can hardly be tackled in isolation unless the international community has the wisdom to assume collective responsibility in order to break this vicious circle of population explosion and poverty. It would be disastrous for the world economy to ignore the assessment of the World Bank and the International Monetary Fund, revealed at their recent meeting that the multibillions in loans and other aid to Third World countries will go down the drain if these countries do not adopt tougher birth control programmes. Population explosion is a sure recipe for ecological disaster as well, because environmental deterioration is as much a consequence of hunger and poverty as it is its cause. "While overpopulation in poor nations tends to keep them poverty-sticken, overpopulation in rich nations tends to undermine the life-support capacity of the entire planet," stated Paul R. Ehrlich, Bing Profesor of Population Studies at Stanford University. The myth that the damage to ecosystems is caused primarily by population explosions in poor countries is not valid because "the birth of a baby in the United States imposes more than a hundred times the stress on the world's resources and environment as a birth in, say, Bangladesh. Babies from poor countries do not grow up to own automobiles and air conditioners or to eat grain-fed beef. Their life-styles do not require huge quantities of minerals and energy." Denuding of the forests, polluting the seas and creating holes in the ozone layer that protects the atmosphere are as great a threat today to mankind's survival as the nuclear Sword of Damocles hanging over its head.

The moral outrage I felt against poverty in India at the time of Independence is not any less today. In spite of the enormous progress that India has made during the past forty years in the fields of agriculture and industry, poverty in India has increased because the population has more than doubled, and it will soon reach the daunting figure of a thousand million people. In a country comprising a third of the world's poor, it is awful to reckon that every 1.2 seconds, an Indian is born, fifty more by the end of the minute, 3,000 by the hour, and by the end of *each* day a multitude of 72,000 are added to India's population. Its catastrophic implications for future generations can hardly be overemphasized. It is indicated by the frustration of *An Unemployed Graduate* (Plate 79), a young man whom I had photographed unaware in front of a government secretariat. The illiterate masses aside, how could the educated youth have any hope for the future when each year India is *adding* to its population, as many people as in the whole of Australia? Until now the pious charade of religious bigotry had prevented

Plate 86: THE *BIDI*-MAKER, KERALA

Plate 87: A CHILD CHOPPING WOOD, UTTAR PRADESH HIMALAYA

Plate 88: A CHILD COLLECTING BRANCHES FOR FUEL, PUNJAB HIMALAYA

even knowledgeable international organizations from speaking out their true assessment of the situation, thus covering up the frightening reality by superficial statistics and make-believe solutions, based solely on effective management, market-oriented reforms and education.

Other factors, such as education, are of course important, but how is it possible in a largely illiterate country to install over a million additional primary and secondary schools annually to cope with its population explosion? I saw the enormity of the problem in different parts of the country as I discovered how small was the number of children in primary and secondary schools. *Children Going to School* (Plate 81) in Kashmir, *Children Going to School* (Plate 80) in Ladakh and *Children at School* (Plate 82) in the Punjab were among the several photographs I had taken. But these did not present the true picture. The reality of the situation was clearly written on the famished faces of two schoolteachers whom I had photographed in Uttar Pradesh and in the Punjab (Plates 83 and 84). The man from Meerut told me of his inability to educate his three children as he could not afford to pay their school fees even though he himself was a teacher in a primary school. There were parents who did not consider that formal education for their children was even essential, as seen in *Father Teaching his Son* (Plate 85). It was a photograph of a grocer in a Punjab village, whom I had snapped as he was teaching one of his six children to count so that he could help him sell his merchandise — sugar, a bag of which he sat upon. His attitude towards his children's formal education was as unfeeling as the flies hovering over them, a hygienic hazard to which he was as insensitive as the priest of the Ranganathan temple was towards works of art.

Child labour was another curse of overpopulation and the resulting poverty. *The Bidi Maker* (Plate 86) in Kerala, was just one example of the numerous unfortunate children who at a tender age were put to work, as was *A Child Embroiderer* (Plate 43) and *A Child Artisan* (Plate 42) in Kashmir. The child making the *bidis* or cigarillos was from a state that prided itself on the highest level of education for its people in the whole of India, and hence it was all the more depressing when he told me that none of his five brothers and sisters had ever had any formal education. Many children never went to school, and any instruction they received was solely for the purpose of their economic exploitation and servitude to which they were yoked by their equally illiterate elders. *A Child Collecting Branches for Fuel* (Plate 88) and *A Child Chopping Wood* (Plate 87) were the forerunners of the environmental and ecological disaster in

Plate 89: CHILD BEGGAR, NEW DELHI

Plate 90: *HARIJAN* CHILDREN, MAHARASHTRA

Plate 91: CHILDREN PLAYING CARDS, PUNJAB

which vast areas of lush green vegetation in the Himalayas have been denuded, thereby causing even more havoc in the plains because of flooding. Poverty- stricken illiterate children became beggars as *Child Beggar* (Plate 89) in New Delhi; or just vagabonds in sprawling cities like Bombay, Calcutta and Madras, as seen in *Children Playing Cards* (Plate 91). Even though as early as 1951, India was the first country to have launched a programme of family planning, the galloping increases in population has also undermined the abolition of illiteracy.

Pandit Nehru never asked me why I did not publish *This My People* until in the second week of January 1964, fifteen years to the day after he wrote the preface. At that time he was convalescing after a stroke that he had just suffered on 7 January, and I frequently visited him at Teen Murti House. On that day he was sitting in an easy chair placed for him at the far end of the rear garden, and seeing a camera in my hand, he was suddenly reminded of his preface to my collection. I could not give him a convincing explanation why it could not be printed, except to say that my other projects had come in the way, as well as my duties in the Foreign Service. I was glad that he had enquired about it, not because it referred to my work, but as a proof that his mental faculties were still sharp, thus kindling my hope that he was on his way to recovery. It created the illusion that his illness was no more than a freak storm that was about to blow over as suddenly as it had started. And his reminder about *This My People* had set me thinking seriously about publishing the collection as soon as it was possible. But unfortunately that was not to be, as Prime Minister Jawaharlal Nehru passed away on 27 May 1964.

Exactly forty years have gone by, and yet it seems as if it was yesterday that I went to meet Pandit Nehru, carrying on my bicycle the collection of photographs which is now dedicated to his cherished memory. It is published to mark the centenary of his birth on 14 November 1989. On that occasion, the preface which Panditji wrote in his own hand to *This My People*, will become a part of the Nehru Museum's collection of historical documents at Teen Murti House, New Delhi, where I had met him on that memorable winter morning in the first week of January 1949.

Plate 92: THE FUTURE OF MANKIND

LIST OF PLATES